God,

Where in the

World Are You?

Devotions for

a Traveler's Heart

Spring Edition

Susan C Howell

God, Where in the World are You?
Spring Edition
Published by Vacations Unlimited Publishing
4091 De Zavala Road suite 3
San Antonio, Texas 78249

ISBN 978-0-9862072-2-8

Unless individually notated, all Scriptures are taken from the Holy Bible, New International Version (NIV) Bible Gateway, on line.

Special recognition to Gary Chapman and his book: "Five Love Languages"

Printed in the United States of America
Volume Two – Spring Edition

2014 First Edition

This book is available for purchase in bulk or volume discounts when purchased by corporations, organizations and special-interest groups. Custom imprinting or excerpting is available to fit special needs. For information and pricing, please email: susan@susanchowell.com.

Due to the nature of this changing world, any locations mentioned in this book may have changed names since publication and may no longer exist by the names mentioned within.

Dedication:

To my Grandmother

Mabel Conklin

As a praying woman, she was my example.

I know she always kept me before

God in her prayers

and I truly believe that she is the reason

I have chosen to follow

Jesus Christ as my

Personal Lord and Savior.

Acknowledgments and profound thanks go to the following:

Prayer covering:
My wonderful husband; David Howell

Scripture research and proofing:
Ben, Sabryna, Jennifer and Rebecca Hawes.

Accountability buddies:
Rosalee Little and Jeannette McNamee

Organizer:
Nora Martinez

The 'team' who read my very rough drafts and critiqued them:
Dennis & Lisa Bonnet, Crissy Galm, Randy & Brenda Garcia, Bruce Henderson, Frank & Rosalee Little, Deana Mobley, Nancy Montez, Laurel Montgomery-Torres, Pete & Sonia Villarreal

Book cover design and graphics:
Melinda Mueller

Of course my editor who pulled it all together:
Dave Yeager

Pastoral Endorsements

"The reason people say 'a picture is worth a thousand words,' is because pictures help us understand something at a deeper level. In these devotionals, Susan Howell paints beautiful pictures to help us understand the depth of love God has for us. Whether it is the setting of Buckingham Palace or the Shepherds Fields outside of Bethlehem, Susan helps us open both our physical and spiritual eyes to see the great handiwork of our Creator."
Rev. Randy Garcia, Senior Pastor,
Fortress Church, San Antonio, Texas

"The beauty and glory of God are everywhere. They are seen every day in every corner of our world. This devotional leads us daily on a journey to discover the wonder of God in the small moments in which we find ourselves along life's journey. Reflecting on the things that can be seen thousands of miles away reminds us to pause and observe the nearness of God on our own path today."
Matt Rule, Pastor, Houston, Texas

"As Christ used life stories, parables, to teach God's truth, Susan uses her true-life experiences in traveling through God's creation to open the reader to the reality of God in life today. As such, the reader will find an exciting way of seeing the truth and presence of God in their everyday experiences of life."
Chaplain (LTC) E. C. "Van" Vanderland
U.S. Army retired

March 1

Alaskan Sled Dogs

One of the main modes of transportation in Alaska is the dog sled. There are competitions throughout the year, with the culmination being the "Last Great Race on Earth®," the world famous thousand mile Iditarod from Anchorage to Nome. When visiting Alaska, a favorite place to visit is the Happy Trails Kennels of Martin Buser. He and his team of dogs have won hundreds of races throughout Alaska, with the highlight being four Iditarod championships.

Martin and his son take time to explain their philosophy in running their business. They are the coaches, and the dogs are the athletes. They feed their athletes a strict scientific diet, designed by Martin, and train them with much love and devotion. Each day – rain, shine, or snow – the dogs wait for their exercise. Pulling a sled is what these four-legged athletes live for; they bark and jump, turning in circles with excitement. Once all of the dogs are in their individual harness, they are off like a shot. Digging in with their tiny paws, pulling on the lines, ears flopping in the wind, this is what they love to do.

Martin and his team of helpers protect the dogs by putting booties on their paws and specially designed thermal blankets on their backs when running on snow and ice to help protect them from frostbite. Seeing the love he has for the dogs and the complete devotion they have for him is amazing and heartwarming. They look to him for everything, knowing he will give beyond what their needs are. When I see Martin's love for his dogs, it reminds me of God's love for us.

Matthew 6:25-26

Therefore I tell you, do not worry about your life, what you will eat or drink; or about your body, what you will wear. Is not life more than food, and the body more than clothes? Look at the birds of the air; they do not sow or reap or store away in barns, and yet your heavenly Father feeds them. Are you not much more valuable than they?

God, You do take care of me! You make sure there is food to eat, that I have shelter, and that I am clothed. Even more than that, You love me. Your love is so much more than the love Martin pours out on his beloved dogs. What You do for me and how much You love me is far above any love man can comprehend. So Father, let me always remember when I begin to doubt, that You DO love me without question.

March 2

Arlington National

Boarding our blue tram at the visitor center, people of all agers, cultures, and lifestyles suddenly work as one. Squeezing over to let a stranger sit or moving to let an elderly person have a more convenient place, there is a bounding, a respect for life here. As we begin our tour, a pre-recorded audio message details information about the most famous cemetery in the world.

Our focus is the Changing of the Guard ceremony at the Tomb of the Unknown Soldier. Stopping near the amphitheater, people quickly make their way to the other side, where the Tomb rests, overlooking the Washington Mall hoping to find a place to sit to view the ceremony. Across the valley below, the Potomac River divides two worlds. On the cemetery side: somberness, sadness and respect for life and Country. On the other side: politics and fast-paced government, highlighted by the stately dome of the United States Capitol building, shining in the afternoon sun.

We choose to stand near the entrance to watch the young men dressed in immaculately groomed detail march past as they exchange positions with the current guard on duty. The men who serve the Tomb must commit two years of their lives to guard it. They will live in barracks under the Tomb and cannot drink any alcohol, on or off duty for the rest of their lives. They cannot swear in public for the rest of their lives and can do nothing to disgrace the uniform or the Tomb...ever.

After completing the two-year commitment, each guard is given a pin in the shape of a wreath, which he wears on his lapel, signifying he served as a guard of the Tomb. By wearing it, he commits to obey the rules for the rest of his life or give up the wreath pin. Less than 400 men currently wear the wreath.

What dedication. What commitment. How I respect these young men. They are the armor bearers of the military. Each man and woman serving in our Armed Forces knows there are men keeping watch at Arlington National Cemetery. Rain or shine, ice or snow, the men keep watch. Night and day, even in blizzards and hurricanes, the Tomb with the bones of unknown soldiers, brought from battlefields around the world, are under tight watch. Never to be forgotten.

Psalm 91:11

For he will command his angels concerning you to guard you in all your ways.

You, God are my protector, my covering, my shield. Thank you for allowing your Holy Spirit to stand watch over me. Your protection is more than the men at the Tomb can ever provide. There are so many times in my life I know You are there, Your angels wrapped around me, keeping me safe in Your loving arms. I praise You, Father.

The Mad King

Sitting on the highest peak in the region, Neuschwanstein is a fairy tale castle for boys and girls, even men and women. Commissioned by King Ludwig II of Bavaria, Germany, it was never completed. The "Mad King," as he was known, lived in some of the rooms for about 172 days, until his sudden death in 1886.

Everyone who has been to Disneyland has seen a modified version of this castle: Sleeping Beauty Castle. Walt Disney was so taken by its beauty; he chose to make it the centerpiece of his park.

The original structure was built using common brick. The outer walls were covered in white limestone and marble. Inside, our guided tour took us into many of the completed rooms. Blue sky could be seen through the lead-glass windows. There are no obstructed views up here.

Climbing from one level to the next, we walk across gray stone hallways and up forest green carpeted steps. Each step of carpet is pulled to the step's inner edge with a golden rod. This prevents the carpet (and us) from slipping. Some of the long hallways echo as our shoes tap out our steps, while other hallways warm themselves under red carpets.

A library fills one room. Hundreds of leather-bound books sit silently behind glass doors. The Hall of Singers has wooden flooring, light wooden boards cut at forty-five degree angles. Heavy red drapes hang beside red and gold wallpaper. I count three Chandeliers with more than one hundred lights on each one, adorning the ceiling.

My favorite room is the dining room. A small square table sits on deep red carpet with only three ornate gold, red and dark wood chairs around it. Gold trimmed paintings cover all four walls. A small white marble fireplace covers the lower part of one wall. The Mad King did not like to have dinner guests. In fact, he preferred to dine alone, so much so that the dining room had a dumb waiter. The staff would load his food on the tray and using a set of pulleys, it would be lifted from the kitchen below to the dining room. He would take the food off when it arrived, and dine alone … completely alone.

As we walked down the steps to return to the main entrance, I begin to wonder how the King must have felt when he finally passed from this earth and he saw the magnificence of heaven. All of the gold and riches one could ever spend can never come close to the glory and beauty of the presence of God. In fact, Jesus tells us that He is preparing rooms just for us in the following scripture.

John 14:2-3

My Father's house has many rooms; if that were not so, would I have told you that I am going there to prepare a place for you? And if I go and prepare a place for you, I will come back and take you to be with me that you also may be where I am.

Father, Your word says You are preparing a room, a mansion for me. I know the Mad King built an amazing palace, but I do not believe it will come close to the glory that I will see when You call me home. I also know that with You as my King, I will never be alone. It's so much more than I deserve on my own. Thank You for giving Your son, Jesus Christ for me.

His Grand Canyon

Wind blew our jackets open as we stepped off the bus. The North Rim always has wind, I think, as I zip up. Log cabins with little flower boxes at the windows are on each side of the narrow road leading to the lodge. Winding around two flagpoles, flying the red, yellow, and blue of Arizona and the red, white, and blue of America, the road makes a circle.

Entering the lodge, thick, heavy, wooden doors open easily. A dining room is off to our right, and the hotel check-in is on our left. Following the crowd, we descend a few steps to the viewing room. Wood benches mix with overstuffed sofas and rocking chairs to provide abundant seating facing a wall of glass. What appears to be a massive painting of the Grand Canyon is in fact, the real thing!

Small, dull green scrub brush cling to the brown desert dirt, stretching as far as the eye can see. Flat on top, the canyon opens wide, eighteen miles across. The deepest point is more than a mile below the rim. A light haze hangs across the valley today, causing the colors of the canyon to appear softer.

Walking outside, I zip my jacket and then quickly grab the handrail, protection from the strong winds. Flat stones have been placed along dirt pathways that snake along the edge of the cliff. Handrails are ever-present and much appreciated. Turning to my left, I choose a path less traveled. After a few minutes of slow walking, due to shortness of breath at this high elevation, I pause. The view is stunning. The world is His!

Psalm 37:23-24

The LORD makes firm the steps of the one who delights in Him; though he may stumble, he will not fall, for the LORD upholds him with His hand.

I am away from the crowd.

Now, Lord ... now it is You and I. I praise You for Your canyon. For the colors of minerals that You have placed so perfectly: greens, reds, oranges, yellows. Each one stretches for miles, laying in flat rows, like a cake with many layers. You put things into perspective. You caused this to be as You wanted it, and You created me. I am your perfection. I am Your glory and beauty. Humbly I thank You for loving me so much. Please let me honor You in everything I say and do.

You Are My Great Wall

There it is! Directly in front of us is the wall, the Great Wall of China. Stretching over five thousand miles, some of the sections date back to 220 BC. Parking our bus, the group prepares to walk a section of this historic wall. Gray stone is stacked over 25 feet high and over 20 feet thick at the base. What an imposing structure! Watchtowers are spaced at inconsistent intervals along the snake-like wall, which hugs the crest of the hills for miles in each direction. Arriving at the upper edge of the wall, I realize that it is only about ten feet wide. Very few sections of the wall have smooth surfaces on which to walk. It is mainly rough, uneven steps of ancient stone and brick.

Some steps are wide and easy to put my foot on, while others are so narrow that only my toes press against the well-worn rock, as I climb to the one above. I can barely stretch my leg high enough to reach the next, while a few steps later they are just inches apart. There is no consistency, as far as the eye can see. Yet it was an important military fortification created to protect the southern part of China.

How does this relate to my life, Lord? The wall winds like a snake for miles in every direction with few consistent sections. At times, my progress is measured in tiny, baby steps. At other times, the steps are almost overwhelming, huge. The wall itself is a divider from good and evil. Warring parties would come from the North to invade China, and the scattered watchtowers were there to sound a warning. Lord, You are my watchtower. You teach me and warn me to know when evil is trying to creep into my life. Just like the wall, which lies like a snake, the enemy tries to slither its way into my life. However, like the Great Wall, you are my protector. You are my defender. You keep me safe as I walk the uneven steps of my life, towards eternity with You.

John 16:33

"I have told you these things, so that in me you may have peace. In this world, you will have trouble. But take heart! I have overcome the world."

Father God, You are my everything. You protect and provide for me, and I thank You. Through Your Holy Spirit, You watch over me and warn me when danger approaches. Forgive me for all of the times I choose to ignore Your warnings and fall away from You. Restore me and guide me into a closer walk with You. I know there will be big steps and little steps along the way; all I ask is for You to continue to hold my hand.

March 6

Hanauma Bay

Standing on the cliff overlooking the bay below, I was captivated; God had painted this picture. There was no other explanation. Green, manicured grass lay under stately palm trees, gently blowing in the breeze. I could hear the leaves rustling, dry branches dangling, waiting for their turn to fall. White sand covered a wide swath from the grass to the small waves tumbling over themselves as they casually aimed for the shore.

How to describe the water: blue, aqua, turquoise? Yes, all three. Coral reefs stretch their fingers along the sea floor, under the waves, creating shadows and reflections, giving the water its various colors. The bay forms the shape of a tight "C," creating the feeling of a private world.

King Kamehameha and Queen Ka'ahumanu; the beloved Royalty of Hawaii in the late 1700's, loved this bay. An invitation by the Royals, who loved entertaining guests here, was an honor reserved for the elite. Today, everyone can dive into the water and swim with over 400 species of fish. The fish come in every color of the rainbow: bright blue with yellow lips; orange striped, like the child's story of Nemo; black and white spotted; and iridescent are just a few of the types we see. Green turtles swim in these waters as well, reaching up to five feet in length. They are as curious about us as we are about them.

Drying off, I sit on my towel, watching others romp and play in the surf. Overcome by the beauty surrounding me, I began to weep. Lord, this is just a small part of Your glory! What will heaven be like? If this is not Your idea of perfection, I can hardly wait to see what is!

Psalm 8:8-9

The birds in the sky, and the fish in the sea, all that swim the paths of the seas. LORD, our Lord, how majestic is your name in all the earth!

Father God, I am in awe of Your greatness. It is amazing to see Your beauty here on earth and know that it is tarnished rags next to heaven. I am so excited to see Your kingdom. Thank You for inviting me. My answer is Yes! I want to follow You.

Hats for Sale

Our ship docked this morning on the sunny island of Jamaica in the Caribbean Sea. It is already hot and humid without a cloud in the sky. Our sightseeing bus has taken us to a beach. We take off our shoes and massage our feet in the warm, white, soft sand. Our next stop will be a small grouping of high-end shops.

Traveling from point to point, the road hugs the shoreline. Sharp rocky ledges reach out into the surf, stopping each wave as it races towards shore. Further along, the beaches stretch their flat sand in a wide welcoming cove.

Our final stop is an outdoor market where the local craftsmen sell their wares. Nothing fancy, just beautiful Jamaica! One lime green shop sells hats. Straw hats. The owner, a tall, dark woman, is wearing a bright yellow shirt over a long, tan and cream checkered skirt, her hair pulled up into a bun. Two young girls sit on three-legged stools, weaving yellow-tan straw in and out, over and under with nimble fingers. Dipping into buckets of water to soften it, it becomes more pliable... easier to create the desired product.

When it is washed and softened, the straw bends easily to achieve the finished product, becoming what the creator had planned. That is how our lives are with Jesus. He asks us to be baptized, dipping us in water, to wash away our sins, making us more pliable, more usable by Him. He has a vision and purpose for each of us. It is much easier to bend into the shape we are meant to be, as we are softened by His water and nimble hands.

Imagine how beautiful we will become, as we allow Jesus Christ to mold us into His perfection, to be used in the way He knows will be best. How exciting to think that the One who created the heavens and earth wants you to be the best you can be! It's easy to do. Ask Him to reshape you. Tell Him you want to be shaped and used by Him. He will take it from there!

Romans 12:2

Do not conform to the pattern of this world, but be transformed by the renewing of your mind. Then you will be able to test and approve what God's will is ~ his good, pleasing and perfect will.

Father, I want to be molded and shaped by You, to be used for Your glory. Dip me in the waters and soften me for Your good. I love You, Lord.

March 8

If You Build It ...

Just like the movie, our bus traveled down the dirt road, turning into the farm. Getting down, I walked over to the corn field. The stalks were taller than me, with long fat ears. We had been planning this event for some time, wanting to create the perfect "Americana" experience for our group.

Lunch was served behind the farmhouse, beside that wide white porch: hot dogs with all of the fixings, potato salad, chips, soda. For desert, apple pie! What else would we have at a ball game? The metal bleachers began to fill so we filed into our seats. Out in the field, an older man spoke to us using a portable microphone. He shared events about the filming of the movie called "Field of Dreams," including the fact that two families owned the property. Paperwork and permission had to come from two lawyers. Each family wanted exclusive rights to the sale of souvenirs so two different types of collectibles had to be created.

Then, the fun began in earnest. Popcorn and peanuts were sold by young boys, until a noise was heard in the tall corn stalks. Players in vintage uniforms came out, carrying their old-fashioned gloves. There were two teams. They took their places on opposing benches. We stood to sing the National Anthem, the umpire shouted out the familiar call, "Play ball!" and we were off. Laughing at their flubs and cheering on "our" team, our cares are miles away. Before long, it is time for the seventh inning stretch. Everyone stands and sways to a recording of "Take Me Out to the Ball Game."

All too soon, it is over. Our bus is back in that long line of tail lights leaving the field. "If you build it, they will come," I heard in my mind. Again, I heard, "If you build it, they will come." What does that mean to me, Lord? What do You want me to build, and who is going to come?

The next morning, I woke up to a revelation going off in my brain: If I build my faith in Jesus Christ, others will come to Him!

Jude 1:20-21

But you, dear friends, by building yourselves up in your most holy faith and praying in the Holy Spirit, keep yourselves in God's love as you wait for the mercy of our Lord Jesus Christ to bring you to eternal life.

Lord, God, I want my life to be built by You. I can't do it alone because You are the author and finisher of all that is true. Thank You for calling me to serve in Your field of dreams, to build my faith where others will want to come and worship at Your feet.

Mud!

Arriving at the Dead Sea in Israel, sitting at 1,400 feet below sea level, which is the lowest elevation in the world, our guide pointed to changing rooms. "Women, here. Men, way over there." As each person changed from street clothes to bathing attire, mostly shorts for the men and shorts with dark t-shirts for the women, we walked over hot sand, down to a wide wooden gazebo.

Towels were dropped on lawn chairs in the shade. Sandals removed, the "hot sand" dance began, as we scurry to the water's edge. No longer tan in color; the sand had become black, soft, smooth mud. Slippery mud. Placing our feet on the damp mud, we slid the short distance into the water. Here we were, an entire group from church, slipping and sliding, our arms flapping the air like out of control birds, laughing with and at each other.

Walking out into the water, our feet still slipping on the mud below, we realized we were floating. The Dead Sea is over one third salt, which produces buoyancy, giving even the non-swimmer confidence to join in the fun. Across the way, a man was sitting in the water, reading a newspaper; he was out too far to be sitting in a chair. We realized that the salt water was supporting him. Deciding to try it ourselves, many of us leaned back, pulling our knees up, and "sat" in the water.

Turning around, I saw that our pastor had covered his upper body in mud. As if he were bathing, he rubbed the soft, dark earth over his arms, chest, and face. According to Biblical accounts, King David would come to these waters as a place of refuge. The cleansing properties of the mud have been documented for thousands of years. Pastor Randy said, "If it was good enough for King David, it's good enough for me!"

Scripture is full of references to the "cleansing powers" of Jesus Christ. Here, at the Dead Sea, we felt the cleansing mud. Mud which King David used for healing. The man who God said was "A man after my own heart." If this man/king could be loved as he was by God, cleansing himself in mud, how much more should we desire the cleansing power of Jesus Christ?

John 14:6

Jesus answered, "I am the way and the truth and the life. No one comes to the Father except through me.

Father, I want to be cleansed by You. I want to feel fresh and beautiful again. Restore in me Your son, Jesus. Help me to have a better relationship with You. I am asking to be washed in the cleansing power of Jesus so You will call me "a person after Your own heart." Thank You, Father.

March 10

One if by Land ...

Good walking shoes on, check. Hat, check. Bottle of water and all the other things I think are important stuffed into my back pack, check. It's time to hit the trail, the Freedom Trail in Boston, Massachusetts.

Last night we mapped our course from the information provided by the visitor center. Our first challenge was to climb the road to Copp's Hill Burying Ground. Here, we discover thin, gray slate markers. Some were easy to read, while others had faded away, lost to the ages. I do recognize one name: Robert Newman. He was responsible for putting lanterns in the steeple at the Old North Church, when Paul Revere took his midnight ride.

Turning left, we look down the hill. Directly in front of us, at the bottom, sits the Old North Church. Red brick covers the majority of the small building. Looking up, we see the famous whitewashed steeple. "One if by land, and two if by sea." Paul Revere made his famous ride in 1775, to warn the men in Lexington and Concord that the British Regulars were coming.

Inside the church, wooden white pew boxes stand in rows, each about six-foot square with high wooden sides, and a door. These were designed to be family boxes. Children could stay "contained" while the family worshipped. Another advantage to the boxes is temperature control. On cold Sundays, families would bring containers of hot rocks or coal. Placing them in their boxed pew, the space warmed quicker than trying to heat the entire building. One pew box still has the original owner's name on it: George Washington. Today, the church is an active Episcopal church.

Leaving the historic house of worship, we pass through a tree-lined cobblestone courtyard. At the far end is a life-sized bronze statue of Paul Revere sitting on his horse.

We saw and learned so many things on our travels today. I wonder how many people plan their lives as well as they plan their vacation. For that matter, I wonder how many people plan for their eternity. Some do not know how. To those people, I say two things: 1. Go to a visitor center, we call them local churches, one that teaches that Jesus is the Son of God, who died on the cross for our sins. He was buried, and three days later, He rose from the dead. 2. Ask Jesus to forgive you of your sins and to come into your heart to live with you.

That is how you plan your eternity. The rest comes, as you get more knowledge about your new best friend and His daddy: Jesus Christ and God the Father.

Proverbs 16:9

In their hearts, humans plan their course, but the LORD establishes their steps.

Father, please help me to make better plans for my eternity than I have so far. Thank You for sending Your son, Jesus, to die for me. I am in awe and excited about Your perfect plans for me.

March 11

Owl's Head

Sitting on a rocky point of land at the entrance to Rockland Harbor, the tiny light house is a beacon for ships entering and leaving the rugged Maine coast. Built in 1826, Owls Head Light is the shortest lighthouse of the fifty seven registered in Maine, standing only 30 feet tall, yet still visible perched on her seventy foot high granite cliff. With a whitewashed brick base and a black stripe near the top, the light can be seen at least 16 miles out to sea. President John Quincy Adams ordered it built to protect ships carrying lime from Maine to the rest of the country. When fog sets in, the horn sounds two loud blasts every twenty seconds.

Climbing the wooden steps to the light, the view was breathtaking. A sailboat with full white sails floated across glass-blue seas. She was the only vessel within our site. Green forests lined the rocky shore. A mix of fresh paint, pine needles, and ocean air tingled in my nose.

Such a tiny lighthouse, yet so beautiful, and so important! She is a bellwether in the storm, a beacon for those who are lost, and a warning for those approaching dangerous rocks.

Jesus Christ is our lighthouse, our beacon, a strong tower. He is beautiful, and He guides us by His light. He is so important in our daily walk. Yes, He even has a fog horn, the Holy Spirit, who warns us when we are too close to danger.

Proverbs 18:10

The name of the LORD is a strong tower; the righteous run into it and are safe.

Father, You are my light. You are my direction. Thank You for giving me Your Holy Spirit, to lead me and guide me, to protect me and focus me. I want to look to You for everything I say and do. Not just for me, but for others, too. I want them to see You in me. You are my strong tower, and I feel safe in Your light.

March 12

Faith in a Foreign Land

When planning tours for groups, I prefer to visit the hotels, restaurants, and other sights before taking my guests, eliminating any surprises. My Pastor and I designed a tour of the Seven Churches of the book of Revelation, all in present-day Turkey. We decided that it would be important to visit Greece, primarily Corinth and Athens while we were so far from home. From Athens, we would board a boat for several days, cruising the Greek Isles to include the tiny island of Patmos, where Saint John wrote the book of Revelation. Our cruise would end in Turkey, where we would travel by bus to the Seven Church sites.

I flew by myself to Athens, where I had prearranged to meet with a gentleman from a local tour company. He carried my luggage to a waiting taxi. Placing my bag in the trunk, I climbed into the back seat. He joined the driver up front, and we were off. The airport in Athens is about 45 minutes from my hotel. It is twilight. Driving along, I was enjoying listening to the men talk (it was all Greek to me!), I realized that I had to have total faith in these men. I could easily disappear, never to be seen again. In my heart, I started thanking God for watching over me and keeping me safe, which He did throughout the tour.

Psalm 121:7-8

The LORD will keep you from all harm, he will watch over your life; the LORD will watch over your coming and going both now and forevermore.

Thank You, Father for protecting me. You are a shield over me and my rock to lean upon. When I am awake, Your angels are around me and, when I am asleep, they hover over me. Let me always walk in Your footsteps because that is where You are. You are my defender and protector.

March 13

Sheepherder

The sheepherder's hand moved ever so slightly as a soft sound escaped his lips. Nearby, a black and white, long-haired dog quickly moved from his position on the grassy knoll to herd the sheep. Large, shaggy, off-white colored creatures with tiny brown faces, they looked like giant cotton balls bouncing across the field. As he silently moved the furry animals in the direction the herder signaled, the dog closely watched and listened to his master. Watching this interaction between man, dog, and sheep, it was easy to see how much the man loved the animals in his care.

Our visit to Ireland included a stop at this location, high on a grassy slope, low stone fences dividing the light green pastureland. Below us, the ocean stretched as far as the eye could see: bright blue turning to foamy white, as it dashed upon the craggy cliffs. Each time the dog heard a slight sound from the master, he would respond accordingly. To the right he moved the sheep, now to the left, then up the hill and then gathering them into the corner of the stone wall. One sheep did not want to go, but the master called in a small voice and the dog left the herd. He went after the wayward one and brought it into the fold.

Jesus is like that in our lives. He loves us so much. He does not yell or speak rudely to us. In a still, soft voice, He calls us, suggesting the direction in which we should go. Like the sheep, we can choose to follow the voice of our Master, Jesus, or we can go our own way. Our comfort comes from knowing that He is always there, watching out for us, making sure we do not slip and fall off of life's cliffs. All we need to do is listen to our Master and follow Him.

Life will not be perfect, we will still have challenges. There will always be the voice of One who loves us, to help navigate the stone walls and sheer cliffs.

John 10: 3 - 4

The gatekeeper opens the gate for him, and the sheep listen to his voice. He calls his own sheep by name and leads them out. When he has brought out all his own, he goes on ahead of them, and his sheep follow him because they know his voice.

Heavenly Father, help me to hear Your still, small voice. I know You speak to me. I just want to hear You more and follow You better. Your way is safe, not along cliffs, but in green meadows. Thank You for loving me so much. You are my Master, and I choose to follow You.

March 14

The Gift

Traveling with a group on an extended bus trip truly brings out the good and the difficult in people. One lady could find nothing nice to say about her husband. He was a quiet man, partly because he could not get a word inserted into her ramblings. She preferred spending time with one of her lady friends more than being with her husband. It made me sad listening to her tell anyone who would listen to her, about how difficult he was to live with. I prayed for her and for an inconspicuous time when I could to talk with her. Finally, on the last day, she started in again, discussing all of her husband's weak areas. This was the opportunity I had been praying for. Would I lovingly confront her, or would I just listen and move on. Saying a quick prayer, she paused in her discourse; I knew God was giving me my window to help her.

Knowing that she professed faith in Jesus Christ, I asked her if she had ever thought what Christ might be thinking about His gift to her. She was complaining quite a bit about that gift, and I just wondered how He must feel. She stopped and looked at me and asked, "Gift?" I said yes, the gift He gave you on your wedding day. She understood I was talking about her husband but did not like the direction in which I was going. I asked her if she had ever read a book called "The Five Love Languages" by Gary Chapman. She had not; I explained that each person has at least one unique emotional way of feeling fulfilled. When you understand these ways and practice them, they will change the relationship.

I pointed out to her that she enjoyed talking. I asked her if her husband liked to talk, also. She stopped and looked at me, paused, and said, "No, I don't think so. He always just sits there so I have to do all the talking." I asked her what he did like. She said, "Nothing really, he has his hobby out in the garage, but that's about all." My next question was, "Do you ever go out in the garage and ask him about his hobby?" "No," she said. "It's boring." "But," I asked, "how do you know, if you haven't given him the chance to share what he enjoys?"

When she got home she bought the book and they read it together. They learned what little things the other needed to feel loved, and how to sow good things into each other's lives. Recently, I ran into her in a social setting, and she pulled me aside. There was a different glow about her, as she whispered the good news of their restored marriage. For years, each of them had tried to fill their own emotional needs by using their own "love language" instead of filling the needs of their mate's. They have learned by fulfilling the other's emotional needs, that person, in turn, is more than willing to be responsive and interactive with them. With God's grace, they are now a different couple.

Ephesians 5:25-27

Husbands, love your wives, just as Christ loved the church and gave himself up for her to make her holy, cleansing her by the washing with water through the word, and to present her to himself as a radiant church, without stain or wrinkle or any other blemish, but holy and blameless.

Lord, let me be open to Your calling on my life. Let me be ready to speak when You want, and ready to see the needs of others before my own.

March 15

Tulum

Bouncing along dirt roads, through forests of tropical trees, our bus finally came to rest in a parking lot. The white lines for parking had long ago faded into the whitish-gray asphalt, which meant cars and buses parked wherever they wanted.

Our guide walked with us onto a grassy field. The soil was more sand than dirt, but what should I expect this close to the Caribbean Sea? We were standing on a small portion of the Yucatán Peninsula, near the Mayan ruins of Tulum, Mexico. Our views were of a tropical forest on one side and the ocean on the other.

An entire village had been excavated: homes, businesses, and a place of worship. The largest and most completely detailed building sits at the highest spot, a rocky point overlooking the sea. Off to the right and down about 40 feet is a white sand beach ... a little cove. There are only two ways to get on and off this beach: the water and the well-worn steps carved into the steep, rocky cliff.

The Spanish came as explorers and occupiers in 1518. Sadly, they brought their diseases with them. The native people had no immunities for those illnesses and were not able to survive. In less than one generation, 70 years, the Mayan people were decimated.

As we left the village, once more bumping along in that old bus, I began to think about the "70 year" thing. In 70 years, an entire culture was gone, wiped off the face of the earth, forever. They had no way to combat their "enemy."

I wonder how many of us have family members who have been taken ill by the enemy and are dying, spiritually dying. We need to stop the clock and take back the years, before all '70' are used up.

How do we do that? What kind of "treatments" do we have that would be soul saving? The first line of attack is prayer. We need to pray for our loved ones. Pray that they will want to be healed of their diseases. Pray that they will come to have a personal relationship with Jesus Christ.

Acts 17:26-27

From one man He made all the nations, that they should inhabit the whole earth; and He marked out their appointed times in history and the boundaries of their lands. God did this so that they would seek Him and perhaps reach out for Him and find Him, though He is not far from any one of us.

Dear Jesus, I ask for Your love to cover my family and friends who do not know You. Please put a desire in their heart to reach out to You. Help them to know that You are the most important part of their lives, and that Your love and forgiveness is greater than anything they can imagine. And Lord, thank You for my own joy that will come when my loved ones will walk with You.

Bone Yards

"Where do old airplanes go to die?" a friend asked, as we were driving through New Mexico. I had no idea what he was talking about, and I am sure that was evident by the look on my face. He repeated the question: "Where do old airplanes go to die?" Having no clue, I said just that.

Before long, he turned off of the interstate onto a road that, judging from the tall grass growing in every crack of the thin asphalt, had not seen many cars recently. There, in front of us, was the most amazing thing I had ever seen in the deserts of the great Southwest: airplanes. Big, huge airplanes. UPS, American Airlines, DC 9s, 727s ... You name it, they were there, acres and acres of planes. As we drew closer, we could see the planes lined up wing tip to wing tip, hundreds of them everywhere. Stopping a man walking towards us, we asked him what he knew about the place. He said that plane bone yards are all over the southern states, from California to Florida. After 9/11 and when fuel prices get too high, companies fly their planes to these fields, storing them until needed again, or in some cases, chopping them up for recycling. He seemed surprised that we were surprised!

What a horrible waste of money, I thought to myself, as we drove back over the grass-covered road. Is my life like that, Lord? Do I take the things you give me, the huge gifts waiting to uplift myself and others, and park them in the desert places of my life? What am I doing with them?

Matthew 6:19-21

Do not store up for yourselves treasures on earth, where moths and vermin destroy, and where thieves break in and steal. But store up for yourselves treasures in heaven, where moths and vermin do not destroy, and where thieves do not break in and steal. For where your treasure is, there your heart will be also.

Father in Heaven; please forgive me for putting aside the things You have given me: the time, the talents, and the opportunities. I really do want to be used by You for Your glory. Thank You for giving me another chance to serve You.

March 17

Birthday Boy

Dublin, Ireland, on St. Patrick's Day is chilly with a light wind. We do not care, as we have reserved seats at the parade about a mile from our hotel. Choosing to walk, we find many of the streets are closed to traffic and filling with people celebrating the holiday.

Since the seventeenth century, the Irish Catholics have celebrated March 17 as the day St. Patrick brought Christianity to Ireland. Now, the festival is celebrated worldwide as a day of shamrocks, rainbows, and leprechauns. The reason behind this special day has, generally, been lost.

People pass by, wearing outer garments of emerald green. Some have green scarves wrapped around their necks, while others have painted green shamrocks on their faces. Vendors push their carts along the streets, stopping to sell their wares to people sitting on the curbs. Green cotton candy, bags of peanuts, toys, and noisemakers are selling briskly, as people settle into their seats. Our seats are next to the reviewing stand, which allows us the opportunity to see each group perform at their best for the judges. There are also two Irish television celebrities providing commentary to the audience.

Irish parades are much different from those in the United States. We have huge marching bands. Today's parade has one. The funny thing is the band is from the United States! They have many acrobatic entries, which are fun to watch. There is a man on a tightrope high above the street, traveling down the parade route on a flatbed truck.

The television commentators excitedly explain to their viewers the details of each entry, as we listen in. During breaks in the action, we visit with them. One of the women in our group whispers something to the celebrity, who laughs and nods her head.

After the parade ends, the two commentators come over to our group. The man takes off his tall "leprechaun" hat, and the woman takes off her green, knitted scarf. They give them to my husband, David and wish him a happy birthday. With much laughter, our group tells us that they had whispered to the woman that today is David's special day.

We had a great day celebrating Christianity arriving in Ireland and the birth of David, who is happily wearing his oversized green hat and scarf. This is a simple blessing for him. I want to treasure this day, to remind myself that the simple things in life are often the best.

Proverbs 17:22

A cheerful heart is good medicine, but a crushed spirit dries up the bones.

Lord, thank You for reminding me how important it is to do little things for others. I want to follow Your example in bringing joy and laughter into the lives of the people around me.

March 18

Well Done?

As a tour director, I call ahead to hotels and restaurants re-confirming our arrival time, the exact number of guests, etc. While touring New England during the fall foliage season, I had called a restaurant where dinner would be served for us the following evening. Everything was ready, the menu was set, and we would be dining on the wooden deck near a river with a nearby covered wooden bridge. This was truly a treasure, as there were no other restaurants for miles in any direction.

I was excited to share this beautiful location with the group and had been telling them about it for several days. The hour arrived and we turned onto the winding dirt road lined with brilliant fall-colored trees. Red, orange, and golden leaves were mixed among the evergreens, bobbing and waving in the gentle evening breeze.

Rounding the last bend, our bus driver came to a screeching halt. There, in front of us, was the picture-perfect wooden covered bridge. Across the lawn, where the restaurant used to be, were smoldering embers from a fire, recently extinguished. What to do? Here we were, almost 40 people, hungry for their evening meal.

The next closest restaurant was at least an hour away, and we couldn't be sure they would be able to feed our large group. Getting creative, we went to a little Mom and Pop store a mile or so back down the road. We cleaned them out of everything we could find for a picnic: bread, cheese, meats, chips, sodas. Taking our booty back to the lawn at the base of the covered bridge, with the smell of the recently burned restaurant hanging in the air, we sat on our newly purchased blue tarps to eat a dinner fit for a king. Well, at least fit for a group of happy travelers.

Matthew 6:26

"Look at the birds of the air; they do not sow or reap or store away in barns, and yet your heavenly Father feeds them. Are you not much more valuable than they"?

Heavenly Father, I know You created me much greater than the birds of the air. I know You watch over me much closer than You watch over each one of them. You protect my steps and provide for my needs. Thank You for loving me and taking care of me, even when I don't realize what You are doing.

March 19

Timing Is Everything

Trees flashed their fall colors at us, as we drive towards the Capitol building in Frankfort, Kentucky. Reds, oranges, and gold mixed with evergreens, created a classic picture of God's handiwork. Beautiful. Breathtaking. Words can hardly define the scene.

Rounding the corner, a long, green lawn, decorated with orange and yellow flowers, leads us up the drive to the main entrance. A maintenance worker buzzes past us on a huge riding lawn mower. The smell of fresh cut grass fills our bus.

Upon entering the grey and white marble rotunda, we are met by our local guide. The building was completed in 1909 and houses all three arms of the Kentucky government. Much of the architecture is of French influence, including the grand marble staircases. Looking up, the dome has several murals of modern and classical design, complete with gold embellishments.

One of our lady guests asked my husband for a wheelchair. She wanted to see the building, but knew she would enjoy it more if she could sit. He found one and brought it over to her. As he approached her, a gentleman standing next to her had a stroke and started to collapse. David turned the wheelchair towards the man, and he sank into it.

EMS arrived in a timely manner and took him to the hospital. The entire thing happened so quickly. The man was taken care of very well and has had an amazing recovery.

We know the expression "timing is everything." How often do we relate that to God? His timing for our lives is everything. He created us in this time, in this century, in this country, in this family for a reason. He created beauty all around us, for our pleasure. Do we stop and realize how much He loves us?

Jeremiah 29:11

For I know the plans I have for you, declares the LORD, plans to prosper you and not to harm you, plans to give you hope and a future.

Lord, thank You for Your timing. I don't realize how perfect it is, and I ask You to forgive me for that. You created me in such detail and beauty. I don't always think I am beautiful, but Lord, when I look at the other things You created, I accept Your decisions. Help me to see others through Your eyes, to see their beauty and Your timing, as well.

The Garden

Smooth, grey stones line the pathway guiding pilgrims down the hill. Off to the left are cemeteries filled with hundreds of aboveground, white tombs, each with a tiny stack of stones placed along the edges. Jewish custom is quite prevalent here. Tiny stones are believed to help keep the spirit from drifting off before the return of their Savior. The One for whom they are still waiting.

Passing a high stone wall covered in green vines, with fragrant yellow and white flowers, we arrive at the Garden of Gethsemane. Standing before us are several rows of olive trees. Silver and grey leaves cover large twisted branches. The diameters of their trunks are wider than a grown man could wrap his arms around. Thick and gnarled bark accentuates their age. They have been carbon dated over 2000 years old.

This was THE garden where Jesus often came to pray. This was THE garden where He came to pray that last evening when Judas Iscariot betrayed his Lord. This was where the disciples fell asleep while Jesus prayed to be released from the pain and separation He was about to face. This beautifully maintained garden across the narrow Kidron Valley outside the walls of Jerusalem is where My Lord talked to His Daddy. Closing my eyes, I shut out the voices of other pilgrims and focus on Him.

Matthew 26:36

Then Jesus went with his disciples to a place called Gethsemane, and he said to them, "Sit here while I go over there and pray."

Jesus, Thank You for loving me so much that You were willing to die on the cross. You teach me so much about Your love and compassion, how to look after others who need You. Let my spirit not be held down under rocks and stones, but let it rise to meet the purposes You have for me to serve others, as You do.

March 21

Didn't Think That One Through

Traveling with a group of senior adults in Washington, DC, we had dinner on a boat on the Potomac River. It was a beautiful clear night. Soft music was playing in the background as dinner was served. The ladies and gentlemen were truly enjoying themselves. During the evening, a lady came to me and said she needed to use the restroom, but they were downstairs and due to her medical situation, she couldn't use the stairs. My husband, David, overheard her plight. He offered to walk in front of her to help her navigate the stairs. She agreed, and off they went.

He waited patiently outside the door. Soon enough, she appeared, looking up at him, ready for him to help her conquer the stairs. He had not thought about getting her back up; he was just proud he had gotten her down!

After thinking for a bit, he came up with a great plan. She was a tiny lady so he bent over and scooped her up, carrying her like a child, as she giggled all the way up the stairs! Before the night was over, she found David three more times to help her use the facilities!

It was such a little thing for him to do for her. Yet it was such a big thing for her to receive such special attention and help. I watched her the rest of the evening as she visited with her friends. She laughed and giggled like a school girl.

I am so glad David was able to help her. Isn't that the way Jesus is for us? He is ready to pick us up and carry us when we need help. He never pushes himself on us, He waits for us to ask...what a gentleman!

1Peter 4:10-11

Each of you should use whatever gift you have received to serve others, as faithful stewards of God's grace in its various forms. If anyone speaks, they should do so as one who speaks the very words of God. If anyone serves, they should do so with the strength God provides, so that in all things God may be praised through Jesus Christ. To him be the glory and the power for ever and ever. Amen

Lord, thank You for loving me so much. Thank You for taking care of the little things. Let me always be like the example of David in this story: ready to serve others with love and generosity, as You have taught me. Let everything I say and do bring light into someone's life and glory to Your name.

March 22

Going-to-the-Sun

Brilliant blue skies, spotted with white puffy clouds cover the heavens, as we climb into long red vehicles called jammers. Originally built in the 1930s for touring Yellowstone National Park, they were brought to other parks as their popularity increased. Brown leather seats greet us as our driver opened all five doors. Settling in, he hands out thick, red and gray plaid wool blankets that will keep us snuggly and warm, as he rolls back the tan canvas roof.

Forest on both sides of the two-lane road creates a green tunnel effect, as we travel the lower elevations of the park. Soon the fragrant pines give way to open space. There, in front of us are the high, rugged snow covered Rocky Mountains. Our driver turns onto the Going-To-The-Sun Road, beginning our ascent.

The narrow, two-lane road, carved out of solid rock, does not have a shoulder or even a guard rail along the outer edge. This is not the place for people who are afraid of heights! With the top rolled back, our long red convertible bus has gone from chilly to amazingly cold! It is obvious why the driver had given us the blankets. Since the top is down, we can look straight up...up to the sky. Nothing grows on this section of rock. It is sheer brown and gray, until it touches the heavens.

The valley is receding with each hairpin turn of the road. Pine trees we had looked up to a few minutes ago are now far below. A river flows below us. Cold and rushing water from the melting snow tumbles over mighty boulders, cascading from cliffs above. Solid rock gives way to steep alpine meadows. Small ground animals bob up and down, as they run across the new growth.

The visitor center at the summit of Logan Pass is waiting, nestled into the hillside, over 6,600 feet in elevation. This is the end of June, and there are still more than ten feet of snow on the ground. The parking lot is filled with cars and long red buses. Inside is a small museum with photos of wildlife and vegetation, warm restrooms, a small gift shop, and more warmth! All too soon, it is time to head further along this ribbon of stark natural beauty.

Pulling into a rest area, our driver invites us to admire a lake. Walking across dirt and smooth boulders, around small trees, the lake appears. Long and slender, Saint Mary Lake lays over a thousand feet below. A small island with pine trees sits near the coastline, begging to be included in our pictures. Before long, it is time to return to our waiting bus and travel the cliff side of the road back to our waiting car.

How amazed I am at the beauty of nature. I try to fathom God's eye for color. It is far beyond me! However, that will not stop me from praising Him for the glory He shows us each day. Look around! He is everywhere!

Psalm 121:1-3

I lift up my eyes to the mountains, where does my help come from? My help comes from the LORD, the Maker of heaven and earth. He will not let your foot slip; he who watches over you will not slumber,

Dear Lord, the heavens and the earth are Your creation. The beauty within it is Yours. Help me to see Your beauty in everyone and everything around me. I want to know You more, to reflect You so others can see You the way I do. Thank You, Father for Your love of all things, especially me.

March 23

Walk This Way

My husband David loves physical exercise. What can I say? Everyone has a weak spot. Actually, it is a quality I admired in him. When we travel with our friends, he likes to invite everyone to join him for a morning walk at 6am. Rarely does he get any takers.

One morning in Deadwood, South Dakota, he was waiting in the hotel lobby, as usual, hoping someone would join him. At about 5 minutes to 6, the elevator doors opened and out walked one of our friends! David could not have been more excited! "Ruben! You came!" Without missing a beat, David turned and led him out the door.

The little town of Deadwood is built in a narrow, steep valley. Evergreen trees cover the surrounding hills, sheltering a clear creek, which tumbles over a bed of smooth, round rocks. Knowing the area well, David led the way up a very steep street, around a corner, and down the next steep hill, while breathing in the crisp, cool, morning air. Up and down the hills they went, Ruben did his best to keep up, his shorter legs having to work twice as fast as David's long ones.

The sun was rising, peeking over the hills to the east, like a floodlight focusing on the green, gold, and silver leaves across the valley. The two men stopped to watch a doe and her fawn nibbling on a bush. Birds were waking, singing a good morning song.

After more than an hour, the two men finally returned to the hotel, with Ruben worn out and perspiring. That was the only time anyone showed up to walk with David. Several days later, Ruben approached David and told him that he had not gone to the lobby to walk that morning. His real purpose was to get a cup of coffee and breakfast. However, he felt so bad when he saw how excited David was, he just couldn't say no!

Are we like that with Christ? Do we have our own agenda, as David did? Are we more focused on our own desires than others? We know there is so much to experience; do we forget to wait on the Lord? Or are we like Ruben who looks at our Lord and sees how excited He is when we follow after His desires? God is excited to share His blessings with us. We need to pause and make sure we are going in His direction and in His timing.

Proverbs 16:9

In their hearts humans plan their course, but the Lord establishes their steps.

Lord, let me always remember that Your steps will lead me to Your perfect plan for my life. Let me not turn to the right or to the left pursuing others' plans and ideas or trying to fulfill my own desires because Your plans are so much better.

March 24

The Porter

During the month of June 1999, I had taken a group of senior adults to Yosemite National Park in California. We stayed at a lodge near the park entrance. The last night we were there, we had dinner on picnic tables around the swimming pool. For some reason, I decided to climb the hill behind the pool and take a picture of the group.

In the morning, as we were preparing to leave, I followed my routine: I stood by the open luggage compartment of the bus, checking off each bag the porter brought from the lodge. We loaded them onto the far side of the bus, away from the view of the hotel and the guests. Having completed that job, our guests boarded the bus, and we went on our way.

The next month, I was at home reading an article in the local newspaper about the killing of a Yosemite National Park naturalist. The man they had arrested was also the man who had killed a woman and two girls in February. Turning the page to continue the story, there was a photo of the accused murderer. It was my porter from the lodge. I had been on the far side of the bus with this man for about thirty minutes. My blood ran cold in my veins. Looking back, I remembered the pool picture I had taken. I found it and have it at my desk. Of all the pictures I have taken over the years that one holds such a deep meaning for me. In thinking about that time, that place, the events of that tour, I realize just how "protected" the entire group and I had been.

Psalm 41:2

The LORD protects and preserves them—they are counted among the blessed in the land—he does not give them over to the desire of their foes.

Father God, thank You for watching over me. I need to remember You are always there, preserving and blessing me. Today, keep this scripture in my heart. I bless You and praise You.

March 25

Foggy Shore

Our small ship sails across the Long Island Sound, off the coast of Connecticut early this morning. Breakfast will soon be ready in the dining room. I can tell by the aroma coming from the nearby kitchen. Pouring a cup of coffee I push open the door which leads to the deck. Warm sunlight greets me. Not hot, just comfortably warm and fresh ... welcoming a new day.

Walking around the bow, I am out of the sunlight. It's much chillier here, in the shadows. Across the calm water, fog is rising. Where we are sailing is clear, the sun is shining, the waters are peaceful. Between us and the shore is a grayish-white fog bank. Occasionally, a building or tree peeks through, showing us where the shoreline truly stands.

As we sail along the coast, the fog slowly begins to rise. Buildings are more visible now through a white veil, defiantly visible. A red and white striped lighthouse peeks out at us, and then hides in the fog. Every few seconds, her horn cries its mournful call. Coming back into view, I see she is nestled on a small pile of rocks resting at the end of a wide sandy beach. She disappears again. We can still hear her.

The lighthouse reminds me of God, our Heavenly Father. He is always present, in calm waters and rough, in clear skies and fog. He warns us when we are near danger. Even though we can't see Him, He is still there. In a still, small voice, He calls out the warning call. It is up to us to listen and make corrections in our course.

John 10:27

My sheep listen to my voice; I know them, and they follow me.

God, You are so good. I worship You. Please help me to hear Your warnings more clearly, to turn from places I shouldn't be, and to avoid people I don't need to be around. Direct me to people who worship You and to places that will keep me from harm's way.

Famous Smile

The glass pyramid is in front of us as we make our way through crowds outside the Louvre in Paris. I knew about this museum as long as I could remember, never dreaming that a child from my poor upbringing would ever see it. Stopping on the sidewalk, I took in the view, imprinting it on my mind. The Palace, dating back to the 12th century, was the original museum, which wraps around the courtyard on three sides, as if to protect the glass pyramid in the middle; the old structures protecting the new.

A couple stands nearby, sipping cups of strong smelling coffee, nibbling on pastries, and speaking French. This was it! I really was here. Inside the museum, sensory overload set in quickly. So many works of art, painted, sculpted, and designed by so many famous artists. The original statues of Nike and Venus de Milo are right in front of us!

There was one painting I insisted upon seeing. The security guard said lines are long to get into the gallery, but I didn't care. Mona Lisa was calling, and I must go to her. The crowd was constant and a bit pushy. As we neared the entrance, men and women from all walks of life and every corner of the planet, some with unpleasant body odors and others with fragrant perfumes, pressed to get into the room.

The crowd pressed tighter; we were in! Handsome security guards stood on each side of the painting, which was hanging rather high, covered in Plexiglas. Was that why she was smiling, I thought with a giggle? Good looking security guards on each side of her?

Here I was, standing in front of probably the most famous painting of a woman in the world: Mona Lisa. Leonardo da Vinci painted her in the early 1500s. Her smile has intrigued people ever since. I could not get enough. Squeezing my way to the far side of the room, I studied her smile. Working my way around to the other side of the room, she was still smiling. Inching my way through the press of bodies, I was directly in front of her. What was she smiling about? What was she thinking, feeling, watching? Finally, it was time to leave. I waved goodbye to her as I would a friend.

Much later, I had settled into my seat on the plane for the flight back to the states. My mind went back to The Smile. Isn't that smile how our Lord is? He is always there, whatever angle we choose to go. If we turn to the right or the left, He is there. If we step back, away from Him, or draw very close, He is still there. He sees so much more than we can, and yet, He loves us so much that He can't help but smile.

Isaiah 55:8

"For my thoughts are not your thoughts, neither are your ways my ways," declares the LORD.

Father God, Your word says You are my daddy. As a parent, I know You look at me with eyes full of love. I know I sin and fall far short of Your perfect will for my life, and I ask You to forgive me. Thank You for loving me and smiling at me, as I learn to draw closer to You.

The Volcano

Driving from Naples, Italy, our driver pointed to the mountain on our left and said it was Mount Vesuvius. From this angle, it almost looked like two mountains with a valley between them. The famous volcano erupted in 79 AD, spewing ash over the town of Pompeii. Wind from the ocean would have blown onshore sending the debris further inland; Pompeii is on the back side of Vesuvius, thus becoming the recipient of the ash.

Since 1738 Archeologists have worked to excavate this massive project. Today, there are still acres of un-excavated portions of this town. Walking over huge flat stones placed in the narrow passages, one has a sense of this busy port city that dates to the time of Christ. Wagon wheel tracks are still visible on the rocky roadways. Sailors came from all parts of the known world, each with their own language, not understood by everyone. Signs and drawings were used to communicate. They had beautiful homes with detailed frescos, public baths, restaurants, even brothels!

Pompeii was not a God-fearing town; she had been neglected for the tangible things of the world. The importance of their material possessions is evident throughout the excavated ruins. There are many examples of man's desires and lusts receiving greater attention than their God. The sin of this town was no different than the sin of the rest of the world at that time. Scripture says that Jesus died to take away the sins of the world. Only a few years after His death, the Romans continued to live blindly in their sin, the power of God erupted on Mount Vesuvius, destroying them and their sin.

Romans 3:23-24

for all have sinned and fall short of the glory of God, and all are justified freely by his grace through the redemption that came by Christ Jesus.

God, I stand before You right now asking Your forgiveness for my sins. Your son, Jesus, died on the cross to wash away my sins, and it is my responsibility to ask Your forgiveness. Wash me white as snow, purify my mind and body. Cleanse me from every thought, action, and transgression that I have allowed in my life. Bless me Father, for I have sinned and am confessing to You my shortcomings. Thank You for healing and restoring me, for bringing me to a new place where I can walk closer with You.

March 28

Can You Kayak?

Our small boat anchored in the Canadian waterways, at the end of a channel called a fjord, which is a narrow inlet carved by glaciers cutting through solid rock. Sheer, steep cliffs spill forth waterfalls, cascading hundreds of feet below, as we float just a few miles from the open sea.

Kayaks of bright yellow, red, and blue sit bobbing on the water, waiting for us to climb aboard and carry us across the icy cold water. This water is the result of a glacier melting; and it is very cold!

Pine trees cover the tops of the mountains while waterfalls pour from openings in cracks and crevices, tumbling over cliffs, hitting rocky outcroppings, causing the water to bounce and dance in different directions down sheer cliffs. Sometimes, it falls as a sheet of water, other times it breaks into little streams—some look like a bridal veil, soft and lacy.

Making my way out into the middle of this mile-wide body of water in a bright yellow kayak, my heart overflows with love of God's amazing world, inspiring me to sing to myself some of the old songs of the Church. Deciding to get a little braver in my adventure, I paddle to the center of the inlet and sing at the top of my lungs. My voice is swallowed by the rushing waters of the many falls, but I don't care, I know One who is hearing and loving me. How glorious it is to be in God's outdoor, open air, hand-made house and worship Him in all of His glory.

Psalm 9: 1-2

I will give thanks to you, Lord, with all my heart; I will tell of all your wonderful deeds, I will be glad and rejoice in you; I will sing the praises of your name, O Most High.

God, You are the creator of all things. I worship You. Let there always be praise on my lips and in my heart, as I walk from day to day with You in my life. I want to know You more and worship You more. I love You, Lord.

March 29

Feathers Flying

Swaying to the gentle motion of our restored 1940s and '50s train cars, rolling along the track, I reflect on an event from last night. On that portion of our sightseeing, our cars were traveling from Boston to Washington, DC, making a stop in New York City. Life was grand: We had our own sleeping compartments, a private dining car—complete with our own private chef—and a dome car. Seeing America's backyard was our goal, and we did just that.

The previous night, arriving 8 hours late into New York City, several of the ladies were disappointed. They had never been to New York and had their hearts set on seeing the Big Apple. Several hours before we arrived, one of the male crew members from the train volunteered to take them into Grand Central Station when we finally got there. Not realizing it would be at two in the morning, we finally arrived. We were surprised to find all of the ladies completely dressed and ready to disembark!

Decked out in high-heeled slippers with fuzz on the toes, bright colored pajamas, feather boas draped around their necks, and big floppy hats in place, they all flocked to the train platform. Into the station they went, up the escalators like a row of ducklings behind their mother duck, with the crew member from our train leading the way. What a sight to see: the ladies clip-clopping across the normally quiet—at this hour—station, with their feathers flying and their hats flopping. Just a group of happy ladies having the time of their lives!

Proverbs 3:27

Do not withhold good from those to whom it is due, when it is in your power to act.

Jesus, let me learn to be more giving. Let me see how I can enrich others' lives. I know there are so many things You do for me; let me give to others, following Your example. What a small thing for this man to do, but such a huge thing for those ladies. Teach me to be more like You and thank You Father for allowing me to grow in Your love.

March 30

Thousand Islands

Sailing the Saint Lawrence Seaway we cross back and forth from Canada into the United States. This is home to the chain of islands known as Thousand Islands. Our boat captain points out unique islands along the way.

My favorite is not one, but two islands very close together. A house is on one, and the owner's studio is on the other, with a white bridge and railing connecting the two. The international border runs right between them. One island is in Canada, and the other is in the United States. There are two flags flying, one on each island: the bright red flag with a white Maple leaf for Canada, and the Stars and Stripes for the USA.

How nicely this seems to work for the owner, being able to choose how they want to live, whose laws they want to follow. On and on, my brain kept thinking of reasons why living in two places at the same time would be a great idea.

My thoughts shifted from all of the positives to the negatives. Who would come if you needed help? You would have to remember which building you were in before calling 911. To whom do they pay taxes? They would have to remember two sets of laws and guidelines for their building codes. Since it is near the French-speaking part of Canada, would they need to speak or read French?

God spoke to me at that very moment. "When you live IN the world, you have challenges and doubts, but when you live in ME, you have an 'easy-to-read' guide called the Bible. You have a teacher who loves you more than any government can or will, a teacher who is there to guide and protect you."

WOW! How simple is that? Follow the teachings in the Bible, pray and follow Jesus, and you won't have to figure out on which island you should live. He has already prepared a place-one place, a mansion-just for you.

Romans 12:2

Do not conform to the pattern of this world, but be transformed by the renewing of your mind. Then you will be able to test and approve what God's will is—his good, pleasing, and perfect will.

Father, Your word is so simple and clear. You want to make my life easier. You don't like confusion any more than I do. Thank You for making a way for me to live on Your "island" and not have to figure out how others expect me to live. I love You, Lord.

Corn Fields

Corn fields cover the rolling pastures of Nebraska and Iowa as far as the eye can see. Green leaves, taller than a grown man, reach for the sun; ears of tasty yellow kernels are ready for harvest.

My mouth begins to water, as I think about this important crop. What kind of corn tastes the best? Sweet corn, of course! Popped corn is comfort food. On the cob, with butter dripping, reminds me of summer. Added to soups and stews, it completes the meal. Corn is used to feed cattle and other livestock, and provide fuel for automobiles, as well.

Just like the corn, we can ripen and look great: do all kinds of wonderful things. It is of no use until you invite Jesus into your heart. He can harvest your sin and replace it with sweet results. You are then ready to be used by God Himself. You become sweeter, nicer to be around. You will have a desire to comfort others who are going through struggles. You will become complete in Christ. How exciting it is to help others draw near and be fed by Jesus, by bringing them to know Him, just as you have done.

Our world would not be complete without corn. It reminds me of our relationship with Jesus: sweet, comforting, life sustaining, complete.

John 4:35

Don't you have a saying, "It's still four months until harvest?" I tell you, open your eyes and look at the fields! They are ripe for harvest.

Jesus, I ask You to forgive me of all of my sins, my wrong thoughts, my poor habits, my bad words, and my inappropriate behavior towards others. Wash me white as snow, clean me and prepare me to be used by You, just like the corn in the field. There are so many things I can do for Your kingdom. Use me to bring glory to You. Thank You for preparing me for the harvest.

April 1

Knock Off

New York City. Just saying the words conjures up so many visions: Broadway productions, crowds of bustling people, world-class museums, Times Square with its unique characters, and of course, shopping. Thousands of folks shop here daily. Many prefer the illegal, or "street," shopping instead of the safe, sometimes more expensive, shops. Several of my ladies decide to purchase from one of the illegal merchants. Not wanting them to go off on their own, I agree to supervise their adventure. I help them find one of the "runners" who will take them off the main street to a back shop where they can purchase certain items like purses and watches. We locate a runner and tell her what the ladies want to purchase. She tells us to follow her.

She led us down an alley, across a street, down another street, and to an intersection. Soon, she got on her phone to tell someone that we were nearby. All of a sudden, she turned to us and said, "I don't know you, get away from me," and completely disappeared. She was gone! Looking down the side street, we saw that the purse shop was being raided, and police were putting handcuffed people into squad cars. Once more, I realized how well we were protected by God, even when we chose to take the wrong path ... the back alley.

Psalm 103:2-5

Praise the Lord, my soul, and forget not all his benefits— who forgives all your sins and heals all your diseases, who redeems your life from the pit and crowns you with love and compassion, who satisfies your desires with good things so that your youth is renewed like the eagle's.

Lord, forgive me when I sin. I know there are so many times I do not realize I am sinning. I ask You to show me so that I may change and ask forgiveness. I praise You for protecting me, even in my sin. You do watch over me and keep me safe. Thank You for loving me.

April 2

Mackinac Island

Crossing the bay in our ferry boat, we race over the rough water towards the island. The hood on my windbreaker is not enough to protect my hair from the wind's force. I think about going below, inside, but why? This is exhilarating. Once in a while, we need to throw caution to the wind, breathe in the fresh air ... and let our hair get messed up.

Ahead of us is Mackinac Island: The tiny little island sitting in Lake Huron, off the shore of Michigan. She is only eight miles around and has a "mountain" that rises 850 feet. She has one main town, which is filled with all of the normal beach town businesses: hotels, boutiques, restaurants, and t-shirt shops. There are two other types of shops in abundance here: bicycle rentals, as there are no cars on the island, and fudge shops, at least seventeen to make your chocolate selections quite challenging.

The wide Main Street of town curves along the shoreline. Since there are no cars, the streets are filled with horse-drawn buggies, bicycles, and people; creating a Disneyland effect: no rush, no worry. A purple and white hotel sits amongst other buildings with bright colors.

My nose is on overload, as I walk down the street inhaling the smells of fresh popcorn, cotton candy, horse droppings, suntan lotion, and of course, fudge! Walking to one end of Main Street, I pass more restaurants and hotels. However, they are becoming less "touristy" as I walk.

In town, there are beaches filled with college-aged young people sunning on towels. Small children are playing in the surf, with parents nearby. The beaches are packed. On the southern end of town, where I have now wandered, a man makes his way across a rocky, empty beach with his small dog. Chasing the lapping surf, the dog runs up and down the wet sand. Pulling a non-functioning pipe from his mouth, the man looks at it, looks out over the lake for a little time, and pokes it back in his mouth.

Mackinac Island, thank-you for reminding me of the importance of slowing down.

Psalm 37:7a

Be still before the Lord and wait patiently for him.

Lord, You speak to me in so many ways. Teach me to listen better to Your wisdom. Help me to step back from life so I can relax and see you more clearly. Thank You for showing me what is important in my life.

April 3

Roswell

Tall, dark-green cacti, fingers pointing skyward, stand at attention, as we travel through the desert of New Mexico. A roadrunner races across the hot asphalt, directly in front of the bus, its long tail sticking straight out and head forward, just like in the cartoons! Our next stop is Roswell. Saying the name "Roswell" conjures up thoughts of spaceships and aliens.

Street lights on black poles, high above the sidewalks, have glass domes, as most towns across America do. But no town, other than Roswell, has painted faces of aliens on them! Shops in the downtown area claim to have information on Area 51, a military base rumored to hold objects from a spaceship crash that supposedly happened near Roswell in the summer of 1947. Tacky souvenirs fill the shops. Alien-head coffee mugs, magnets, and the ever popular t-shirt are a few of the wares displayed in windows. Even McDonald's sells their hamburgers from a silver spaceship. It is interesting to see how the town has taken advantage of its unique place in history.

Once we are back on the bus, I watch the desert pass by. How amazing it is to see an entire town so caught up in the "space" thing. I wondered how different it would be if those same people would get that focused on the Lord. Would their shops be filled with t-shirts and mugs encouraging people to live God-fearing lives? Would the buildings look like an ark, a temple, or maybe even a basket hidden in the Nile River?

We all face "aliens" of some type in our lives. Some look like people, while others take the shape of situations. It's easy to feel out of control when the 'space ships' of life attack. We don't have to have our lives decorated with things we can't control, when we have the creator of Heaven and Earth right here. He loves us so much and has given us the ability to choose to follow Him.

Philippians 2:9-11

Therefore God exalted him to the highest place and gave him the name that is above every name, that at the name of Jesus every knee should bow, in heaven and on earth and under the earth, and every tongue acknowledge that Jesus Christ is Lord, to the glory of God the Father.

Father, Your love is so complete. You have led me into a life that is worth living. I know there are times I wander off into other places, doing other things, but You are supremely faithful. You patiently wait for me to return to You. I bow my knee to You and profess that You are my Lord.

April 4

Room in the Inn

Every December, one of the churches in our area hosts a reenactment of the town of Bethlehem at the time of Christ's birth. It is very well done, encompassing an entire city block. The town's people bring live animals, including camels and sheep, while the church members dress in period costumes from the time of Christ. Buildings have been built from wood and grayish-brown brick materials.

Wandering around the town together, my husband and a friend of his stopped to watch the blacksmith hammer out a red-hot horse shoe. A little further down the dirt street, they watch teenagers learning to dip candles. A pot of wax hangs over an open fire as the strings are dipped in and out of the hot bath, then dipped again to add another layer.

Around the corner, in a wooden enclosure the camels chew on hay. Huge beasts of burden with a strong, unfavorable aroma to match! The men discuss how difficult it must have been to ride one of these animals for days and days in the hot sun: not quite what we are accustomed to using for transportation these days.

Roman soldiers stroll throughout the town, stopping to speak to each other or intimidating a peasant girl scurrying by. Some reach into storefronts and take whatever suits their fancy: a loaf of bread, a piece of fruit, or a clay cup from the shelves of the potter.

On the edge of town, they come to the Inn. It was constructed like the rest of the buildings in town, a simple wood and mud-brick two-story structure with four sleeping rooms, two upstairs and two down. Simply furnished, the room held straw-filled mattresses on wood-framed beds. A water basin and rough cloth towel finished off the items in the room. No nightstands or dressers.

Upon leaving the inn, our friend turns to my husband and says, in jest, "no wonder there was no room in the inn, it only had four rooms!" One of the residents of the town, a young lady passing by, overheard the statement. Not missing a beat, she turns to the men and says, "But kind gentlemen, as you can see, Bethlehem is but a small town and does not need a large inn" and kept walking!

What fun to be a part of this re-enactment! To see and hear examples of life at the time of Christ's birth. God's word is quite clear that He has gone before us to prepare a wonderful new place for us to dwell. No shortage of rooms with Jesus!

John 14:2 (KJV)

In my Father's house are many mansions: if it were not so, I would have told you. I go to prepare a place for you.

Thank You, God, for sending your Son. Let me always remember that my King of Kings lived so simply. I don't want to complain when I have little, because with You I have plenty. Your word tells me that You are preparing a mansion for me.

April 5

Eye of the Needle

Ponderosa pines cover the rolling mountains as far as the eye can see. Deep green needles are offset by the dark, almost black, bark of the tree trunks. Granite rock formations peek out from the forest. Some are tall and stately, while others are low, appearing to tumble over themselves.

Motorcycle riders love to travel these mountains. The air is clean, clear, and fresh. Roads are well-maintained, but not straight and wide. These are narrow two-lane ribbons of asphalt, winding their way under the tall trees. Deer roam freely, stopping to watch over their shoulder as we pass by. Two fawns with white spots on their rumps playfully ignore us.

The Black Hills are the guardians of "nature," "Native American culture," and "American history," in this tiny southwest corner of South Dakota. Mt. Rushmore is here. Granite faces of four presidents carved into the side of a mountain are a symbol of American history and patriotism.

Home to the Lakota Indians, the Hills are a spiritual center. The tribes have chosen to carve a memorial, many times larger than Mt. Rushmore in honor of Crazy Horse, an Oglala Lakota warrior who led the war party at the Battle of the Little Bighorn.

Winding our way through the scenic road called Iron Mountain Road; we arrive at a wide turnout. Cars and bikes are parked at odd angles. People of all ages and nationalities, with cameras in hand, are scurrying back and forth. Their focus is on an outcropping, a slender, eroded granite pillar, over forty feet tall with a three-foot-long slit near the top. It looks like a sewing needle, thus its name: Eye of the Needle. Wind, rain, snow, and heat chiseled this formation. God's hand at work!

Matthew 19:24

"Again I tell you, it is easier for a camel to go through the eye of a needle than for someone who is rich to enter the kingdom of God."

Lord, sometimes You create the most amazing visuals. I can see what You mean about the eye of the needle. No matter how few dollars I have, I am still rich. Sometimes, I am too rich in pride. I know I can get too rich in ego, as well. There are so many ways I am too rich to go through that eye, to enter Your Kingdom. Bless me Father; help me to focus my riches on You, instead of the world. Thank You for teaching me how to draw closer to You.

April 6

Reeds on the River

Our boat plies the muddy Nile River. On one side is the large, smoggy metropolitan region of Cairo, Egypt. Buildings with unfinished rooftops display tall pieces of rebar, like fingers pointing skyward. It is customary to leave the buildings in an unfinished state for tax purposes; the building is never finished. Families plan for the young people to marry, and a new level is added for the next generation.

Trash fills the gutters of broken sidewalks, while dogs run wild, with no one to clean up after them. The Muslim call to prayer is heard five times a day over harsh-sounding loudspeakers. Children without shoes play in parks with no grass, while motor scooters and tiny trucks and cars race by. Millions of people live here while several million more live in the suburbs and travel into Cairo for work, then back to their homes at night. Crowded, busy, dirty.

Across the river is the Giza Plateau, home to the Sphinx and the most-recognized pyramids in the world. Centuries of questions and theories exist about how the pyramids were built and for what purpose they were constructed on this exact location. Our boat turns south towards the dock. Snuggled along the sandy shoreline is an area of bamboo-like plants. Deep green stalks with brighter green leaves, the plants gently sway in the moving water. Our guide says it is a stand of reeds. My mind races, as I recall the story in the Bible of baby Moses being placed in a basket amongst a stand of reeds, here on the Nile, hidden from certain death.

God protected that little baby so long ago. He had a plan and a purpose for his life. God has a plan and a purpose for my life, too, although it may not feel like it, as I deal with all of my challenges.

What about Moses' mother? She had some serious challenges! The Pharaoh had ordered all Jewish baby boys to be killed, and she had just given birth to a boy. She placed him in a watertight basket in reeds along the Nile River, to hide him. Pharaoh's daughter found him and decided to adopt him as her own. That would have been another big challenge for Moses' mother.

How did God handle this? He had Pharaoh's daughter ask the Jews to provide a woman who could nurse the boy. Moses' own mother got the job and was able to keep him as a baby and teach him his faith before giving him back to the daughter. Later, as a grown man, he returned from Pharaoh's courtyards and palaces to lead the Jewish people out of Egypt.

Exodus 2:8-10

"Yes, go," she answered. So the girl went and got the baby's mother. Pharaoh's daughter said to her, "Take this baby. Nurse him for me, and I will pay you." So the woman took the baby and nursed him. When the child grew older, she took him to Pharaoh's daughter, and he became her son. She named him Moses, saying, "I drew him out of the water."

Lord, Your word tells me over and over again how much You love me, and You have a perfect plan for my life. Thank You for loving, believing in, and trusting me more than I believe in myself. Thank You for the challenges, not for the hard part, but for what I become as a person, as I learn to trust You more each day.

April 7

Francis

Traveling from Rome, Italy, our little bus made its way north. Turning to the east, the two lane road becomes narrow. Low fencing holds back fields of tall grass and wild flowers. Off in the distance, a village looks like it has been stuck on the side of the mountain. Soon the road narrows even more, as we began the climb to that village: Assisi, Italy.

A fortified city on a hill best describes Assisi's outer appearance. Drawing closer, we see a thriving yet ancient community. Founded almost 1,000 years before Christ, it was built, conquered, and built up again. For centuries, it has seen peaceful times, full of planting and harvesting the silver/gray olive trees growing across the hillside. At other times, it endured devastating wars ... most of which were in the name of "religion."

In the late 11th century, Francis was born into the wealthy home of a silk trader. During a battle in 1204, he was captured and made a prisoner of war. He had a vision, which changed his way of life. In fact, it changed his outlook on the wealthy. Upon his release, he returned to Assisi, denounced his wealth, and started the Order of the Poor. He also founded the Order of the Poor Clare; a women's version of the Order of the Poor. He was never ordained as a Catholic priest, yet he is considered one of the most venerated religious figures in history.

All Christian denominations share his love of Christ. He introduced the Nativity scene to the world in 1223, and went to be with his Lord in 1226. Two years later, the Catholic Church proclaimed him to be a Saint. One of his more profound statements has been a life example for me: "Preach the Gospel at all times, and when necessary, use words."

Matthew 25:35-36

"For I was hungry and you gave me something to eat, I was thirsty and you gave me something to drink, I was a stranger and you invited me in, I needed clothes and you clothed me, I was sick and you looked after me, I was in prison and you came to visit me."

Jesus, I am hungry, and You feed me Your word. I am thirsty, and You let me drink from Your well. I am not clothed, yet You cover me with Your love and protection. I am in a prison of fear, shame, and guilt, yet You have already broken the chains. I praise You, Lord.

April 8

Old Ironsides

What a glorious day! The sun is shining, birds are singing, flowers hang in baskets from light posts throughout town. American flags of all sizes fly from makeshift holders, windows of businesses, permanent poles, and tiny wooden stakes, stuck into the green grass, along the sidewalk. It is the Fourth of July in Boston. Brunch is waiting for us on our chartered boat. As we climb aboard, music by John Phillip Souza is playing, welcoming us to an American patriotic adventure. Setting sail, our captain explains what would be happening over the next several hours.

We would sail around the harbor, viewing other ships while we ate. At a specific time, the captain would position our boat in a predetermined location, allowing us to see the star of the day's activities: the oldest commissioned Navy vessel in our fleet, The U.S.S. Constitution. Named by our first president, George Washington, she was launched in 1797.

With four tall white sails and over 40 cannons, she is quite impressive. Her nickname, "Old Ironsides," was earned during the war of 1812. British ships lobbed cannon balls at her, but none were able to penetrate the hard surface of her hull, which is made of pine and southern live oak. Instead, they bounced off of her, thus earning her the name.

Every July Fourth, she sails out of her berth in the Navy shipyard across the harbor, performing her "under way" demonstrations. This includes firing her cannons toward Fort Independence, which sits on Castle Island. The fort responds with cannon fire. Smoke from the cannons is visible from our vantage point on our boat. After the demonstration, tugboats turn Old Ironsides around and return her to her berth, to rest for another year.

The harbor is filled with boats of all shapes and sizes to watch the "turnaround." Yachts filled with well-dressed men and women played loud, patriotic music. Medium vessels, like ours, turned up the music, as well. My favorite was a rowboat with two teenagers and a portable stereo. This is Independence Day in Boston!

A modern Navy vessel is anchored nearby. As Old Ironsides approached, "all hands on deck" was called. Navy whites stood at attention, saluting their senior ship. What a sight to behold; the "Rock" of the United States Navy honored and respected with dignity and class.

Is this how we treat Jesus? Do we stop what we are doing and give Him all honor and respect? Or do we keep Him off in the distance...only to be visited when it works into our schedule.

Ephesians 6:10-11

Finally, be strong in the Lord and in his mighty power. Put on the full armor of God, so that you can take your stand against the devil's schemes.

Lord, You are my God. You are my teacher. Help me to have thick skin, to prevent the attacks of the evil one, to have things bounce off of me. I want to be known and respected as one who follows Your teaching, one who learns to withstand the enemy. Thank You, Father for Your abundant love.

April 9

Win-Win

Our sleek red and white riverboat had sailed from Nuremberg, Germany a few days ago. Overnight, a light snow dusted the upper deck, covering lounge chairs. The crew tells us that it is early to get this much snow; a hard winter is projected.

The winter season is why we are here. December in Germany means Christmas Markets ... and this is December! Each day, we arrive in a new town along the Danube River, giving us many opportunities to explore new markets. There are similarities in all of them: wooden booths placed side-by-side in the town's square, music playing through a PA system, food, and hot wine sold in unique mugs.

The big difference in each location is their merchandise. One town is a center for woodcarvers, most everything for sale there is made from wood. In another town, the ladies work delicate needlepoint patterns into linens. Still another focuses on children's toys.

Today, we visit the college town of Passau, in Bavaria, Germany. Before we go shopping, our guide takes us to a large bakery. Two men, who have the classic "German look": solid stocky frames, round bellies, long curling mustaches clinging to smiling faces, greet us warmly. We are here to watch them make strudel, which is a flaky crusted dessert, filled with sweet sauces and fruit. They make and roll the dough, encouraging us to participate. Apples are the filling of choice today. As the finished product is taken away to the large ovens, we are offered a small strudel and a cup of coffee. "Now this is the way to plan your day," I think to myself ... dessert before shopping!

Enjoying the present before enjoying the future: Two chances to win, like our relationship with Jesus Christ. We get to meet Him here on Earth, learning about His life as a healer and protector and His death on the cross, where He took our sins away. Then we leave this Earth and spend eternity with Him in heaven. Win-win!

Have you asked Jesus to come into your heart? If not, He is waiting for your invitation. Talk to Him like a friend, and ask Him to forgive your sins, to make you a new person on the inside. Welcome Him into your heart.

John 14:6

Jesus answered, "I am the way and the truth and the life. No one comes to the Father except through me.

Jesus, my life with You is such a win-win choice. I have You beside me now, walking with me. I feel Your peace and know You are watching out for me. I also know, that one day, I will leave this Earth and meet You in the heavens. That will be my final "win," as I spend forever with You.

April 10

Covering the Bases

While sitting underneath large grayish-green olive trees on Mt. Carmel, we read the story of God showing Himself through fire. We worshiped Him as we sailed the Sea of Galilee, remembering how Jesus had walked on these waters, inviting Peter to have faith enough to walk to Him. The Via Dolorosa was crowded with other pilgrims following the last footsteps of Christ, before his death on the cross. Communion at the Garden Tomb where Jesus died and rose three days later, was a spiritual highlight.

Pastor asked the group to share what had prompted them to go on this particular journey. Why the Holy Land? Several said it was to see the places mentioned in the Bible. They wanted to be able to "see" the places as they read His holy word. Others said it was to experience the culture, to get to know how the Israelis lived, how they dressed and moved about in their day-to-day lives, how they operated their businesses and lifestyle.

One lady said she had studied the religions of Buddhism, Hinduism, and Islam and was now covering the rest of her bases with Christianity. We prayed with her and for her. For the rest of the trip, we showed her God's grace and mercy. She realized that the last religion she was learning about was where she would find true peace. I believe her prayer for salvation came from deep within and was welcomed by the angels on high!

Psalm 96:3 (NKJV)

Declare His glory among the nations, His wonders among all peoples.

God, You are my God, and I will worship You always. Let me learn more about You, as You continue to show me people who need you. Allow my way of walking and talking to glorify You and be an example for others to see You. Create in me a pure heart, one focused on Your will for my life. Thank You for calling my name and putting it in the Lamb's Book of Life.

April 11

Under the Sea

Today, we visit the tiny island of Curacao, which rests only forty miles from the South American country of Venezuela. Mother and I are enjoying a cruise of the Caribbean, and this is our next port of call. She wants to see the beautiful colored fish and coral reefs today, but she is now eighty years old and has not been swimming in over twenty years.

I locate a mini-submarine with easy-to-climb steps and clear viewing areas. Arriving just in time to board and get comfortable, we are excited to find that each seat faces its own glass window. This will provide a comfortable way to watch our undersea adventure. Several families with young children join the already seated group. Their enthusiasm is contagious. One little girl, with matching bows on her pigtails, excitedly reminds her mother to watch for Nemo.

Soon, we are off. Fish of many sizes and colors swim past our windows. Tiny gray ones swim in a large school. They zip one way, dart another, and then disappear. Royal blue fish with big yellow lips mingle with others painted in black and yellow stripes. Marshmallow white bodies with bold orange stripes pass bright yellow fish with blue-trimmed edges.

Some are thin, swimming like a dinner plate standing on end. Others are almost as big and round as a basketball. I sit and study this "other world" sliding by my window. It is mesmerizing to watch the seaweed gently swaying and the colorful fish floating in and out.

As we turn back to shore, I think about this part of God's creation. It is not a normal part of my thoughts when I praise Him for His mighty works. I forget how much detail He put into the sea creatures and their submerged world. He did create each plant, fish, and mammal, which exists here, just as He created all of us. Thinking about the beautiful fish, I have to pause. He created each of us more beautiful than them. I repeat that thought: In God's eyes, I am more beautiful than all of the colorful fish.

We are His pride and joy. He created the Earth and all of the plants and creatures before He created us. We are His crowning achievement.

Psalm 145:3-5

Great is the Lord and most worthy of praise; his greatness no one can fathom. One generation commends your works to another; they tell of your mighty acts. They speak of the glorious splendor of your majesty— and I will meditate on your wonderful works.

God, You are amazing. I sit here thinking about Your plan for this world, and I am so humbled. I know You created me to worship and give all honor and glory to You. Your greatness is so much more than I can imagine. I love You, Lord.

Cycle of Life

Touring the wilderness of Denali National Park in Alaska, bouncing over dirt roads, one experiences a part of life not witnessed by many people. Wildlife roam freely in their natural rugged environment. Our guide, a national park ranger, has lived in the area all of his life. We learn to spot the animals, which blend into the rocks and bushes, stopping to watch them as they interact within their habitat.

A baby falcon sits preening on an old tree stump, oblivious to the ground squirrels scurrying below. His feathers stick out at odd angles, reminding me of my son's hair in the morning. Along the road is a herd of shaggy, long-haired mountain goats, nibbling on the alpine vegetation.

Moose own the road. They walk where they want, and do not back down to things bigger than themselves. What a thrill to watch a 6-foot-tall brown bull moose with huge antlers walk in front of the bus. Two baby moose, less than 6 hours old, are in the bushes nursing from their mother.

In the distance, a mother brown bear plods across a plateau as her cubs run and tumble behind her. Her head is constantly turning from right to left and back, watching, encouraging, and protecting her little ones. Nature is so perfect, so timely, and so complete. I get to thinking about my life. When things are not what I think they should be, why do I doubt or worry? I need to remember that God is turning His head, watching in all directions, encouraging and protecting each of us.

Genesis 1: 25

God made the wild animals according to their kinds, the livestock according to their kinds, and all the creatures that move along the ground according to their kinds. And God saw that it was good.

God, You created it and said it was good, why should I doubt? Lord, forgive me for doubting. Let me trust You more each day. As I look at Your creation, remind me how much You love me and are taking care of me.

April 13

Tiramisu

Tall green cypress trees stand at attention, like tin soldiers, as we make our way down the dirt road. Off to the right are rows of neatly trimmed vineyards, marching over the rolling hills. Off to our left are more rows, but these are olive trees with leaves of silver-gray. Sitting on top of the hills are yellow and soft-orange homes. This is the heart of Tuscany, Italy.

Our hotel is in Florence, about forty five minutes away. The change in scenery is dramatic, quite a contrast from the narrow city streets, filled with bustling crowds, small cars, and motor scooters racing down ancient roads. Country lanes give way to peaceful, romantic farming communities, the kind you see in the movies. Our destination is just ahead on the top of the hill. The classic yellow villa, dating back over 300 years, is still owned by the original family and includes a cooking school.

As we leave our bus, a pair of dogs come bounding up to greet us. Sniffing our shoes, they determine that we must be okay because they turn and leave as quickly as they arrived. Our hostess arrives, beautiful Stephania, with long dark hair pulled back in a clip and classic Italian features. A hint of her native tongue spills into her English as she welcomes us, inviting us to sample some wine or punch, while our chef prepares for our class.

Pasta is made for the ravioli. We put white goat cheese mixed with seasoning onto the dough in little piles. The top layer of pasta is placed over our little piles, and we learn how to cut them properly. After preparing a few more courses, the ingredients are brought out for our grand finale: tiramisu! Our chef shows us how to dip the long slender biscuits into very strong coffee, with just a twist of the wrist. We place them in a baking pan and add the other ingredients. When the pan is full, there are plenty of unused biscuits left over. The chef encourages us to dip and scoop to our taste buds' delight. What fun we have licking our fingers when it is time to clean up.

Later, I got to thinking about Jesus. He has so many lessons for us to learn about doing things the correct way. What fun it is when we do things according to His plan. The blessings of tasting His sweet victory are eternal: our salvation. He has prepared a table for us that we will get to enjoy upon our arrival in Heaven.

2 Timothy 1:9

He has saved us and called us to a holy life, not because of anything we have done but because of his own purpose and grace. This grace was given us in Christ Jesus before the beginning of time,

Father, I think about all of the things You have taught me. I ask Your forgiveness for the rebellion I have gone through and the lessons I have not wanted to learn. Help me to forgive myself because I know that You have already forgiven me. Thank You for the unconditional love You have for me. Let me always learn from Your example.

April 14

Celebrate!

Wengen, Switzerland sits on a ledge of rock fifteen hundred feet above the valley floor. It is a car-less village, which means the paved narrow streets are as safe as the sidewalks. Goods and merchandise are moved by small hand truck or golf-cart sized vehicles. It is a safe little town to explore, any time you like.

This afternoon, the air is clear. Little white clouds perform a slow dance overhead. Little shops line the street: the butcher, the bakery, the Swiss knife shop, and my favorite … the fudge shop. In the distance are the Swiss Alps. To be exact, when you exit the fudge shop, the three peaks are the Eiger, the Mönch, and the Jungfrau.

Several of my friends and I are walking down the main street, heading away from the city center. Behind us, we hear a commotion. The street is filled with people: locals, not tourists. Men and women of all ages are walking together, talking and laughing.

At the front of the crowd, a man is pulling a yellow cart, the kind they use to carry bales of hay. He is dressed in a suit, with a white shirt and dark tie. There is a fresh pile of hay on the cart. Not a bale. It appears to be loose straw with a thin mesh covering, to give it a pillow shape. He is pulling the three-wheeled cart behind him as he walks, and we realized there is a bride sitting on the straw. Her white dress flows around her, lying in fluffy folds on the yellow "throne," her veil gently flowing behind her curled blonde hair.

The wedding was over; the groom was carrying his bride to their home. How simple. How sweet. How visual. The groom was pulling the weight; she was in the driver's seat!

There will be another wedding, soon. This time, the bride will be you and me. Our bridegroom is Jesus Christ. He will come when He is finished preparing our heavenly home. Can you imagine how incredible that will be?

Revelation 19:7,9

Let us rejoice and be glad and give him glory! For the wedding of the Lamb has come, and his bride has made herself ready. Then the angel said to me, "Write this: Blessed are those who are invited to the wedding supper of the Lamb!" And he added, "These are the true words of God."

Jesus, I know You are coming soon to take me home. I am part of the body of believers who You call Your bride. The thought of living with You forever is awe inspiring. Please help me to grow closer to You as I await Your return.

April 15

Peacocks

Strolling the grounds of the old chalet in the Loire Valley of France, a peacock drags his long flowing feathers ... his train. He owns the place. You can tell by his confident walk. A child approaches the bird and is instantly chased away. His coloring is classic: shimmering, iridescent royal blue chest and matching crest on his head.

His train reaches about five feet behind him. Studying his feathers, I am once more amazed by God, the creator of this bird. Each of the feathers has distinct coloring along its length in the shape of an eye, which are difficult to see when he is walking. As if on cue, the bird turns his back to us. With a whirr of his feathers, they rise off the ground, and fan out in a stunning display.

Still whirring, the peacock struts in a full circle. He lifts one leg high, slowly placing it forward and down. Then the other slowly lifts, making sure we all see just how beautiful he is. Once satisfied that we are in complete awe of his beauty and importance, he lowers his tail and returns to pecking the ground for food.

"WOW, Lord! Am I like that Peacock?" Do I strut around making sure I stand out in the crowd? Do I have to have the newest, the flashiest, and the fanciest of everything? Do I have to be in charge, not letting others use their gifts and talents? Do I do these kinds of things even in small ways?

Proverbs 16:18-19

Pride goes before destruction, a haughty spirit before a fall. Better to be lowly in spirit along with the oppressed than to share plunder with the proud.

Father God, teach me Your ways. I don't want to be haughty or proud. I want to be humble and useful for Your kingdom. Show me the beauty You see in others.

April 16

Contentment

Abraham greets us at the edge of his tent. It is a large structure, covered with woolen blankets of gray with thin colored lines of dark red and green. Three sides are down, blocking the sun from baking the interior. Tree trunks, a foot in diameter, stand at intervals to support the structure. Mats of colorful designs in woven wool lay scattered on the floor. The entrance faces the Judean desert in Israel with the Moab Mountains of Jordan in the distance.

Our host is wearing a cream-colored robe with thin blue lines at the edges of the sleeves and hem. Sandals of leather protect his feet from the hot sand. His handsome trimmed white beard accentuates a profile of Jewish heritage. Greeting us as we climb from the backs of camels, he holds a tan-colored clay pitcher of water. Pouring it over our outstretched hands, he refreshes us.

We move into the tent and settle onto thick mats on the floor. The meal is served. New foods are offered. They look much different than our usual fare. Everything is very tasty; in fact, seconds are offered ... and accepted. Abraham wanders through the tent. He stops to visit with everyone and answers questions about the Bedouin, or tent dwellers, and their lifestyle. He talks about how they follow their herds of sheep as they search for food.

The people eat off of the land and are peaceful neighbors. Using the wool from the sheep, they weave fabric for many uses: blankets, camel blankets, tent coverings, and clothes. It's a simple, but hard life. A chosen life. There are towns and villages nearby where one could escape to live. They don't. This is their life. They are a content people.

Sitting on my mat on the floor, I am content. It is cool here in the shade. My tummy is full. My friends are chattering and laughing around me. Yes, I am content. A still small voice asks me if I am content in my relationship with God. Sitting up straight, I look around. Lord? Yes, Lord. I have grown content in You. I have received your grace and Your love.

Philippians 4:11.
I am not saying this because I am in need, for I have learned to be content whatever the circumstances.

Jesus, You have made a way for me. You have blessed me with a peace I never knew existed. You cover me from the cold and protect me from the burning sun. Food is provided for my nourishment. I know You have even prepared a home for me in heaven. I am content in Your loving arms.

April 17

Mountain Stream

Huge boulders lay in the river bed. Winter snow has melted in the mountains above, and water levels are now returning to normal. Trees and other debris, which have been washed down from upper elevations, cling at odd angles to those boulders and outcroppings, reminding me of the child's game of pick-up sticks.

Smooth, polished over centuries, these rocks are an important part of the river. Helping to block large items from traveling downstream, they also provide opportunities for fish to "climb" or "jump" up river. Plants grow in clear calm pools, while fish lay their eggs, protected by the rocks. Mother Nature has an amazing way of using her power for good and bad.

We know the term "Mother Nature" is not a part of the deity; she is not her own existence. She is a part of God, the Father's plan for Planet Earth. She really isn't even a "she!" It is simply a convenient way to describe God's hand in nature, the same hand that created each of us. He still holds out His hand for us to take, to walk with Him as a child would. He is waiting for us to reach up. His stream is a stream of living waters. His stream flows from His heart into ours. He is waiting for us to reach out to Him and step into that awesome stream.

Psalm 18:2

The Lord is my rock, my fortress and my deliverer; my God is my rock, in whom I take refuge, my shield and the horn of my salvation, my stronghold.

Lord, You are my rock, my protector. You are my comforter. You are my haven in troubled waters, and You nurture me, encouraging me to grow and be useful. Thank You for calling my name. I want to be used by You, to help others be fed, comforted, and protected, as You do for me. I love You, Lord.

April 18

Better Idea

"Watch out, watch out," a short man is hollering in a deep voice to anyone who will listen. He is standing on a corner of two cobblestone streets in Oia, on the Greek island of Santorini. Walking towards this little man with the big voice, we try to figure out what we should be watching out for. As we reach him, our answer appears: mules. Ten or twelve mules clomp down the steep stone street toward us.

Leading the way is a young, olive-skinned man in jeans and a gray t-shirt, with a thick blue rope in his hand. The rope is attached to the first mule. Each mule is attached to the one in front, forming a long line. Thin brown saddles rest on dark blue blankets on the back of each animal. It is the end of their day, and they are headed to their stalls, away from the center of town.

All traffic stops while the beasts of burden cross both streets. For those of us who are tourists, this seems so odd, stopping cars and people for a slow-moving row of animals picking their way over the cobblestone roads. While we stand there, we discuss other options for the young man and his mules. They could wait for the cruise ships to leave, taking hundreds of people with them. They could go down the street near a sidewalk, reducing the interruption.

Listening to the discussion, I wondered if that is what we sound like to God. He has a plan and a purpose for our lives. How often do we think we have a better idea? We sometimes think that maybe if we just do it our way, He will see how clever we are! The reality is that it is much easier when we give up on our ideas and let the One who created the heavens and Earth lead us in a perfect direction.

Isaiah 55:9

As the heavens are higher than the earth, so are my ways higher than your ways and my thoughts than your thoughts.

God, lead me where I need to go and keep me from people and places I should not be near. I confess that I do try to do things my way, and I ask You to forgive me. Thank You for showing me how to follow in Your son's footsteps.

Joy Ride

Chicago is full of unique architecture and interesting history. Having only a few hours to explore, we decide to see the sights from the local city bus. In our town, the local bus makes a loop of the city so wherever you get on, sooner or later, you can get off at the same spot. The Chicago city bus is a one way ride!

Boarding the bus, my husband David had been joking with the driver about us living in Texas. Now, we are off. What a blast! We sit in the back row of the bus watching people as they get on and off, and noticing the changing scenery as the bus heads further south. High-rises gave way to small homes; many boarded up or run down.

Finally, the bus was empty, except for us. The driver called out, "Hey Texas, where are you going?" "On a joy ride," we replied. He said we were in an unsafe area and needed to stay with him until he could get us on a bus going the opposite direction.

Soon enough, another one came along, and we climbed aboard. As we traveled back to "downtown," I started thinking about what we had done. We had gone off in our own direction, without thinking about the consequences, not knowing where, just excited to try something different. Looking for adventure, we ended up having to rely on the driver to bring us to safety.

Realizing that I sometimes head off in my own direction in my walk with Jesus causes an ache in my heart. How often do I get an idea

and decide to follow it instead of God? I wonder how many times He looks at me and shakes His head, saying something like, "Here you go again!"

1 Corinthians 10:13

No temptation has overtaken you that is not common to man. God is faithful, and he will not let you be tempted beyond your ability, but with the temptation he will also provide the way of escape, that you may be able to endure it.

Father, forgive me for my lack of focus. Help me to lean on You more and not be drawn away by the worldly things that entice me. I know in my heart that Your ways are the best, and I want to be in Your arms, protected from danger. Thank You for loving and leading me in Your will.

April 20

Cliffs of Moher

In County Clare, Ireland, a stone tower stands. O'Brien's Tower has stood here since 1835. In wind, rain, cold, and heat, the round gray stone tower has stood its ground. As the highest point along the rugged Cliffs of Moher, she stands over seven hundred feet above the crashing Atlantic Ocean, providing guests with an unsurpassed view of God's wondrous hand.

We have been blessed with clear weather today. However, there is still a mist hanging over the cliffs. The mighty Atlantic slams her waves into the rocky cliffs below, producing a continual spray of fine water, keeping the air moist. Trees do not grow on the sides of the cliffs; there are no ledges wide enough for roots.

Visitors come to the tower for views of stark beauty: the deep blue ocean smashing into the cliffs producing white waves that look like whipped cream. Rocky gray cliffs rise to meet green grass, which covers the top of any ledge that will hold soil. Sea breezes provide air waves for the hawks and seagulls to glide across the sky, while the fresh smell of salty air is inhaled deeply. I feel overwhelmed. This rugged beauty has been seen by countless numbers of people for thousands of years. God has allowed me to see another one of His masterpieces.

The cliffs were named after an Irish fort, which had stood where the "modern" tower now stands. There is evidence that the fort,

Fort Moher, stood soundly on this spot as early as 1780. Now, looking out to sea and down the coastline, drinking in the beauty of the cliffs, I stop. It is time to visit with my Creator.

Psalm 46:1-2

God is our refuge and strength, an ever-present help in trouble. Therefore we will not fear, though the earth give way and the mountains fall into the heart of the sea,

Father, You, only You could create this rugged beauty. I see Your hand at work: the surf splashing, the birds flying, and me, yes, me. Your mighty hand is at work in my life, just as it is here in Ireland. I'm asking for Your direction for my life. I need You to remove me from things that will dash me into the cliffs of life and to be my watchtower, warning me when danger approaches. Thank You for Your many blessings.

April 21

Zion

Crossing the sandy high-desert of Utah, we arrive at a bottleneck in the two-lane road. A tunnel appears out of the flatlands, where we have been traveling. The ground has become rockier ... but a tunnel? Traffic is tightly controlled at the entrance; the rock was carved many years ago, before modern vehicles were built so tall. Now, buses and trucks must travel in the middle of the road so they do not scrape or get hung up on the rocky sides.

It is finally our turn. Driving slowly, headlights become the only light. About halfway through the tunnel, two large openings have been carved into the rock. As we pass the "windows" we see a massive canyon stretched out below and a tall mountain with rock outcroppings on the other side. We are descending into Zion National Park.

Upon exiting the tunnel, sunlight greets us once more, revealing that the road we are traveling has changed dramatically. Sharp steep curves lead to sharper and even steeper curves, as we twist our way towards the valley floor. No more hairpin curves! Dark red rock walls on each side are so tall that we can't see the top from inside our vehicle.

Within the park, trams are provided for easier viewing. They provide commentary of the area. Boarding our tram car, we are soon underway. White-barked Aspen trees shake their green round leaves in the gentle breeze. A river tumbles over smooth, round boulders. Sheer cliffs are on our left, reaching almost a half mile into the sky. The other side of the road boasts grassy knolls, hiding behind tall evergreens, which lead up a wash, toward more sheer cliffs.

Rock climbers have been spotted about half way up the flat face of stone. Climbing from our little cars, we gather in a tight crowd. Suddenly, there are no strangers; we are focused on the women or men hanging by thin ropes to the side of the mountain. Several pairs of binoculars appear and are passed around. Those with good cameras zoom in. Sure enough, there are three of them, two men and one woman. They are sitting on an outcropping, high .. very high. Their feet are dangling over the edge, as they eat a meal. It appears as though they have no worries.

In an instant, I see a vision of the difference between how God sees our lives and how we view ourselves. From the perspective of those of us on the tram, we look at the dangerous position of the climbers. We fear living on the edge of life and how easily life can cause us to fall. From God's eyes, he has given us a most spectacular, beautiful, fun-filled life, something to live for, to enjoy! The climbers were doing just that, casually enjoying a bite to eat, drinking in the beauty around and below them, as Christ wants us to do.

Psalm 16:11

You make known to me the path of life; you will fill me with joy in your presence, with eternal pleasures at your right hand.

Father, forgive me for not taking a good look at the amazing things in my life. You have blessed me beyond measure, and I want to take full advantage of all You have for me. Thank You for Your creation, for allowing me to see You in the trees and rocks. I love You.

Answered Prayer

Visiting San Diego, California, we stayed at a beautiful, historic hotel on Coronado Island. As we were loading the bus and preparing to leave, one of the guests had a heart attack. Emergency personnel rushed him and his wife to the hospital, where he was quickly stabilized and placed in ICU. Some of our guests wanted us to stay behind to be with them, but we could not, as we had an itinerary which we needed to follow. After making arrangements with the hotel for the wife to stay, everyone on the bus bowed their heads and prayed for them before we went on our way. Our prayers were answered in several ways.

The hotel allowed the wife to stay in her room and provided transportation for her to and from the hospital, each day. When the husband was well enough to fly home, the hotel staff packed the couples' belongings, drove her to the hospital, and waited while she got him discharged. They helped him get settled in the hotel shuttle and drove them both to the airport.

Each day we called the wife to see how her husband was progressing. The group was overjoyed and at peace to hear how well they were being treated. When we got the good news that he was well enough for them to fly home together, we celebrated. I began to think about how easily unforeseen circumstances can abruptly change our plans.

How quickly something can happen in our lives or even TO our lives. Are we prepared to deal with sudden changes to our health or other traumatic challenges? There is One who is waiting to walk with you through those events; His name is Jesus. He is waiting for you to invite Him into your heart, to have Him guide and support you, as you deal with life. Pray to Him, and invite Him to dwell with you ... He is patiently waiting.

James 5:16b

Pray for each other so that you may be healed. The prayer of a righteous man is powerful and effective.

Father, I know my footsteps are watched by You. I know You have my loved ones in Your precious hands, as well. Allow me to be used by You to help others, as this couple was helped by the hotel staff. Let this story be a reminder that things may appear small to me, and yet are so big to someone else. And Lord, thank You for all of the people who have gone out of their way to help me.

Her Web

Visiting Boise National Forest in Idaho, we park the car and prepare to go exploring. Morning sun has just crept over the horizon. The dirt path is still wet with dew. Each step we take leaves a dark imprint on the ground. It is clear that we are the first to visit today. Forests are similar across the country, yet each one holds its own mysterious uniqueness. This one is no different.

Deep into the woods now, the sun has not plunged her golden fingers through the branches, yet. There is light in the area, but not direct sunlight. Stopping to tie my shoe, I look at the round leaf bush beside me. Near the top, stretched across several leaves, is a perfectly round spider web. Please understand, I am not a spider fan. I have an agreement with those who live near me ... if I don't see them, they can live!

This one catches my eye. She is a big spider, about the size of my thumb. Her web has an incredible amount of detail in it. Each ring is perfectly round, connected to the next ring by perfectly placed cross pieces. Now that sun has found this area, I can see it move a little as the spider tiptoes from strand to strand. Droplets of dew glisten from the creation before me. I stand here mesmerized ... by a spider! I see God here. He is the creator of perfection.

God created the spider and each of us. He gave this spider the ability to spin exactly as she has done, and He has given each of us special talents as well. The spider climbed to the top of the bush and created a

web that glistens in the morning light. We should take this example and apply it to our own lives. What can you do? What gifts and talents are you using for Him? Everyone has them; we need to make the conscience choice to honor Jesus by using the gifts He gave us.

Psalm 37:4-6.

Take delight in the Lord, and he will give you the desires of your heart. Commit your way to the Lord; trust in him and he will do this: He will make your righteous reward shine like the dawn, your vindication like the noonday sun.

Father, You are amazing. You placed that beautiful web for all to see. It shines in Your morning light. I want to use my talents for others to see too. Show me the things I need to do. I want to use them, Lord.

April 24

The Float

Our ship docked in Costa Rica on a clear morning. We had been sailing for several days so the salt air was an accustomed smell. Walking the length of the ship, the wooden pier underfoot, we found our bus transportation. "Old school buses," I thought to myself, as we boarded and found seating. "Leather seats that had seen way too many behinds," I thought to myself, as I settled into my sunken seat. Soon enough, we were bouncing along asphalt roads filled with potholes. Barefoot little children played alongside the road, stopping to wave as we passed by.

Arriving at our "loading area," our guides invited us to sample some fresh papaya juice before climbing into large rubber boats. Donning our life vests, we were pushed away from the sandy shore.

In just a few minutes, our world changed. No buildings, no vehicles, no signs or sounds of civilization. Vines with huge leaves were draped over tall trees, wrapping their grip around anything in their path. Heavy underbrush prevented us from seeing very far into the forest. Tropical flowers of red, purple, yellow, and pink showed off their colors in the bright sun. We were in the jungles of Central America. A screeching noise brought us to attention. Up ahead, high in the trees, white-faced monkeys swung from tree to tree by their long tails.

As we continued our float, wild parrots appeared around the next bend, wearing brilliant colors of royal blue and bright yellow with long feathered tails, calling out to each other as we passed beneath. Our guide pointed off to the right of the boat. Not making a sound, an alligator had swum to a sandbar and was climbing out of the water with his stubby legs. After getting into his preferred spot, he settled in: time to sun himself.

All too soon, we reached the end of our trip, and returned to our big ship with memories for a lifetime and photos to match.

Genesis 1:20, 21b

And God said, "Let the water teem with living creatures, and let birds fly above the earth across the vault of the sky." And God saw that it was good.

Father, when You created the heavens and the earth, I know You created the wild animals as well. I never realized how beautiful this world is. Thank You for Your creation. I know that You created everything with a plan and a purpose, and I am part of that plan. Thank You for making me beautiful too.

The Breakers

Sitting back, across rolling, immaculately groomed lawns of soft green, the home faces the open blue waters of the Atlantic ocean. Her beauty defies description. Designed and built as a summer cottage for Cornelius Vanderbilt II and his family, this home called "The Breakers," was completed in 1895.

Seventy rooms occupy over 65,000 square feet of living space, with indoor and outside fountains, a grand marble staircase, and long marble halls, all completed in great detail by artists using soft muted colors. Everything is accented by gold. Gold paint is used around the fountain trim, with more gold on furniture and fixtures. Paintings larger than a normal sized room are detailed in gold paint.

Giant area rugs, more valuable than the average house, lay protected in rooms only visible from doorways. The room where the nanny lived was closer to the children than the parents' rooms. Dishes, hand painted, with gold trim, sit in elegant settings upon a dining table over twelve feet long. This truly was the life of the upper crust at the turn of the last century.

The wealthy Mr. Vanderbilt had a summer cottage built. He lived as if money would buy him anything. Sadly, he only enjoyed this mansion for four years. A cerebral aneurysm took him at the young age of 55.

Walking across the grassy lawn towards the cliffs and ocean far below, I began to think about this man's life. How amazing that he would invest all of that time and money into a summer home; a home the family would only visit for a few months each year. I wonder if he spent much time and effort investing in his eternal home and if he had a relationship with Jesus Christ, the One who is building a mansion in heaven, just for him.

How many people spend their lives planning, preparing, and building their lives and don't include God? What is their end purpose? What can they expect to receive from it, after they are gone? Sure, it is nice to leave a legacy, but what about the person himself or herself?

2 Corinthians 4:18

While we do not look at the things which are seen, but at the things which are not seen. For the things which are seen are temporary, but the things which are not seen are eternal.

Lord, Your word tells me to prepare and plan for the future. It also tells me to use wisdom for the coming day. I do not know when You will return or when you will call me to heaven, but I want to be ready for that day. Thank You for keeping me focused on things above, instead of things that will burn in fires, here on earth.

April 26

Giddyup

Our goal in life is to follow the teachings and examples of Jesus Christ, how he interacted with people and led them out of their negative past and brought them joy. It is said that we will never know how many lives we touch, until we get to heaven.

Our group was touring the pine forested mountains of Nevada, home to the Ponderosa Ranch movie set, which was used for the filming of the old television series "Bonanza." Keeping the feel of the early western days, our tour was led by men in chaps and spurs. We explored familiar-looking log cabin buildings, the Cartwright's home, as well as Hop Sing's kitchen.

Outside, near the front porch, was a hitching post with a life-size statue of a horse. It was there for effect, to make the area seem more authentic, and to provide a great photo stop. Anyone could climb into the saddle and have their picture taken. Since many of my senior adults had grown up on a ranch, they decided to have some fun; some sat side saddle, while others sat backwards, whatever hit there funny bone.

One lady very quietly asked if she could climb on the horse. The staff of the ranch helped her tiny little frame up on to the large metal animal. She smiled for the camera and then began to softly weep. She sat there with tears running down her face. Finally, she said she had always wanted to ride a horse but had been afraid because she was so small. It was such a little thing for most of us, but for her it was a life experience.

Later, I began to think about that cute little lady. All of her life, she had chosen to stay away from something because of fear. How many times do I stay away from something that looks fun or interesting because I am afraid? Do I do that with God? Sadly, I do. In some things, I don't trust Him enough to believe that He will take care of me completely. I feel like I have to be in charge.

God loves us more than we can ever guess. I know that, as I trust Him in some things, I can look back and see how He took care of them.

2 Timothy 1:7

For God did not give us a spirit of timidity, but a spirit of power, of love and of self-discipline.

God, please help me to trust You more. I want Your spirit of power to take care of me so that I can do more things for You.

April 27

What a View!

Along the cliffs of the Columbia River Gorge, east of Portland, there is a rock outcropping called Crown Point. Sitting on the point is a round multi-story structure called Vista House. She is aptly named: views upriver and down stretch for miles. A cold wind blows as we leave the parking lot and climb her steps.

Once inside, the ground level splits her wall space with tall windows and cream-colored marble, glowing in the morning sunlight. Hand rails and door knobs are of shiny brass, freshly polished to greet a new day. The main hall is cavernous. Our footsteps echo in the quiet, before crowds of visitors arrive.

Climbing to the upper level, I pause to zip my jacket. It's going to be windy! This early in summer, it is still chilly. Opening the door, I find I was right; cold wind slices through my jeans. My hood blows off, tossing my hair to the wind. Turning my back, I regroup and then walk to the front of the building, to the vista, or viewing area.

"It is worth coming," I think to myself. The wind has blown the mist and clouds out of the river's gorge. Our view is clear all of the way to Beacon Rock, which is over 15 miles upriver. I find it interesting that these two prominent rocks are mentioned in the travels of Lewis and Clark, dating back over 200 years. Their surveying party traveled in canoes up this river, describing land formations for future travelers. Today, I stand on top of this solid structure, looking from this rock all the way to the other.

This is a perfect example of our relationship with Jesus Christ. He is our solid rock. He has not moved. He remains fixed, where we can find Him at any time. Jesus is the Rock, the foundation of our faith. Just like the detailed maps of Lewis and Clark, the Holy Bible is our detailed map to heaven. Pick it up, and spend some time following the road map to heaven.

Psalm 18:2

The LORD is my rock, my fortress and my deliverer; my God is my rock, in whom I take refuge, my shield, and the horn of my salvation, my stronghold.

God, You created the Earth, as well as everything in it and on it. You put those rocks there to help guide me, to keep me from getting lost. I know Your word in the Bible is the same way. Please lead me to Your rock ... Your son, Jesus.

April 28

It's Not What You Know

Cairo was not what I had expected, as we bounced over roads full of pot holes, heading for our hotel. The streets were dirty, dusty, trashy, and filthy. Gutters were filled with discarded soda cans and milk bottles. Little children played with old milk crates and car tires in the run-down park. No wonder our tour company had included a gun-carrying escort!

In the morning, the Muslim call to prayer blasted from loudspeakers on tall, slender minarets from mosques all over town, jolting me awake. It was not soft and melodious, but loud, sharp, and annoying to ears that had never heard this call. Five times a day, the loudspeakers blast the message to the 'faithful': stop, get on your knees facing Mecca, and pray to Allah, the god of the Muslim faith. Sending a simple prayer to my God, I thanked Him for the freedom He gives me to worship wherever and whenever I want.

Our day of touring included a tour of the three main Pyramids of Giza and the Great Sphinx. Huge stinky camels waited near the side of this ancient limestone monument. Climbing into the saddle, my camel jerked forward, then back. I was now ten feet off the ground! Each camel had a lead for the handler to hold, while he walked us around the plateau.

At one point, my handler asked if I would like him to take my picture with my camera. Sure, I said and handed it down to him. We posed, he clicked. We did it again for good measure. I reached down to take my camera back, and the man said, "Ten dollars." Not understanding that he was charging me money to get my camera back, I asked, "What?" He repeated, "Ten dollars." Then it clicked in my head what he was doing. Looking up, I saw our gun-carrying escort. Calling his name and waving my arms, I got his attention. He did not say a word. He took two steps toward me, placed his hand on the gun in his waistband, and stopped. My little handler could not get my camera to me any quicker! Here, lady! Take it, take it!

Our Lord is watching over us just as our guard was doing. He is there to protect us from the evil which is around every corner. His watchful eye never loses sight of us and He is ready when we cry out to Him.

Psalm 50:15

"...and call on me in the day of trouble; I will deliver you, and you will honor me."

Father, You are my guard. You have my back. In fact, You have my front and all my sides as well. When the enemy tries to come after me, I just call out the mighty name of Jesus, and You are there. Thank You for watching over me and protecting me from harm.

Let There Be Light

Traveling north from Texas on private train cars, we were required to overnight in Chicago. Sometime after we had gone to bed, the yard engine had moved us into the barn-like building to inspect the underneath side of the cars, which includes the axels, wheels, hoses, etc. It is a huge building with a pit underneath, similar to the kind auto shops use to change the oil in a car. Awaking fairly early, one of my guests decided he would take his shower, not realizing we were over the pit and that the shower water was not contained ... it flowed directly out of the drain onto the workers below. About the time he was lathered up, a light appeared from the drain: it shown bright and moved around, as if to search him out.

He grabbed his towel and ran from the shower room into the dining room, which by now was filled with folks enjoying the morning meal. Standing there, covered in soapy bubbles, wearing only a towel, he froze. After many comments and much laughing from his fellow travelers, he turned and raced away. Later, we were told the water from his shower had poured out of the drain onto the hard hats of the workers below. One of the "hard hats" had taken his bright beam flashlight and shone it up the drain, thus causing the hysteria from our guest.

In our daily walk, are there times we are oblivious to things going on around us and not focusing on anything else but "me?" Do we focus on ourselves, our personal wants and desires, not thinking how our actions will affect others? We often focus on the "I wants" in the world. Just like the men working in the pit below the car, someone can get "rained on" by our actions.

Matthew 6:33

"But seek first his kingdom and his righteousness, and all these things will be given to you as well."

Lord, shine Your light on me. I want others to see me with Your glow all over me. Allow me to become the person You intended me to be and think about others, instead of myself.

April 30

Southern Campaign

Dark green trees cover the hillside of Kennesaw Mountain. Today, there is a national battlefield Park at this location, with well-maintained roads to focus drivers on different parts of the park. Atlanta was the sight of tragic losses during the Civil War. Many homes were burned and destroyed, animals were killed or stolen, and families were torn apart. This was the story throughout the country. There was much sadness and despair in both the North and South.

Visiting this battlefield, which was so much a part of the South, it is difficult to see that tragedy took place here. Old-style wooden fences criss-cross green pastures. A woman in work clothes trims red rose bushes as a coworker buzzes past on a huge lawn mower, the smell of fresh grass following close behind. This is now a memorial with areas to rest and well maintained walking and bike paths. During the Battle of Kennesaw Mountain on June 27, 1864, the North lost over three thousand men. As I stood in the courtyard of the visitor center, I looked out across the green flat land. General William T. Sherman knew this would be a difficult battle and said, "War is hell." I think no truer words have been spoken.

There is sadness in the air, an understanding of tragedy. Throughout history, there have been battles. Many of them were for God's people. His word does not say to avoid conflict; instead it says to love our neighbors.

Mark 12:29-31

"The most important one," answered Jesus, "is this: 'Hear, O Israel: The Lord our God, the Lord is one. Love the Lord your God with all your heart and with all your soul and with all your mind and with all your strength." The second is this: 'Love your neighbour as yourself.' There is no commandment greater than these."

Heavenly Father, I know it is not going to happen that all men will lay down their swords and love each other. I get it. Your son, Jesus, died on the cross, fighting my biggest battle for me. He died for my sins, to keep the evil one from taking me to the pit of hell. Thank You for teaching me to love my neighbor. Let me be an example around my family, my coworkers, and my community of Your love.

Rocks Cry Out

High, black wrought iron fencing hides behind a vine of pink Bougainvillea. At the gate, a weathered sign is photographed, as a remembrance of our visit. The gate stands open, inviting everyone inside. Guards in their Israeli military uniforms mingle with the tourists at the entrance to Capernaum, the hometown of Saint Peter, a fishing village for centuries. The blue waters of the Sea of Galilee are visible through tall stands of palm trees.

Passing dark freshly raked gardens, we pass unearthed flat round stones with round holes in the center. These were used for grinding products, such as olives and grapes. Ancient marble and stone columns lay along the path's edges ... benches to rest upon. The ornately carved bases and caps are placed for resting and photographing.

Excavation has uncovered the stone remains of many shops and homes close to the well-preserved ruins of a synagogue. The Synagogue. Tan stones stacked one on top of another, over twenty feet into the air, still stand. Columns of marble once held the roof and now only hold visual images from the time of Christ. Marble stones cover the floor and seats where one can pause and contemplate the stones all around them.

We know Jesus taught in the synagogues in this area. We know he spent time in this town. It is not difficult to believe that He stood on these marble stones, touched these same marble columns, and sat on these marble seats. He would have been teaching the stories we read today, the examples we choose to follow. Even the stones cry out that Jesus was in the area we are now seeing.

Luke 19:40

"I tell you," he replied, "if they keep quiet, the stones will cry out."

Lord, let me boast about You and Your mighty works. Let each person I meet have a clearer picture of You. I don't want to keep quiet about You because Your love is overwhelming.

May 2

The Agreement

A small group of church friends were traveling in Italy. We had left the excavated ruins of Pompeii, which had been buried by ash and debris in 79 AD, and were returning to Naples to catch our train for Rome.

We would be arriving in Naples well before our scheduled departure. Knowing that this area is not safe for tourists to explore, we asked our driver to give us a tour of the port city. Though he spoke little English, he agreed. He said he couldn't tell us things as a guide would do, but he could drive around and point out famous landmarks.

The radio was broken in the little bus so one of the ladies began to sing softly, praise music mostly. Others joined in, singing softly, as well. Soon the entire group had added their voices: singing loudly. The driver did not know the songs, but he felt the joy we were sharing.

Arriving at the train station with over an hour before departure, we told our driver we were not ready to leave his bus yet: it was too much fun. In his broken English, he said, "If you continue to sing, I will drive you around Naples until you need to be back at the station." Laughing, we agreed. Off we went, bouncing over pothole after pothole. Each person came up with a song; some were praise songs, some secular. "Wheels on the Bus" was sung with as much enthusiasm and volume as "Jesus Loves the Little Children."

Our driver smiled and laughed right along with us. Finally, as we were returning to the station, Dee Dee, one of our women with a gifted voice sang "Alabaster Box." It was so moving. We parked the bus and sat in silence, as she finished. No one wanted to leave.

Finally, it was time. Many of us wiped away tears before collecting our bags. The door opened, and we stepped out of the bus. Each was greeted by our driver in true Italian style, with a hug and a kiss on each cheek. Even the driver's eyes were red and moist with emotion.

What fun we had; our sides hurt from laughter. Sitting on the train, heading back to our hotel in Rome, we talked about our adventure. We had been to Pompeii. We had seen so much history. It was interesting, but our joy was ministering to a little Italian bus driver, we would never see again.

Philippians 2:3-4

Do nothing out of selfish ambition or vain conceit. Rather, in humility value others above yourselves, not looking to your own interests but each of you to the interests of the others.

Lord, help me to be sensitive to Your nudging, to know when I need to speak out and when to be quiet. Let me learn to be bold, to say what needs to be said. I want to learn to say what You want me to say, not what I think needs to be said and let me share Your joy with everyone with whom I come in contact.

Old Faithful

Pulling the car into one of the last empty parking spaces, far away from the walkway, we grabbed our cameras, locked our doors and jogged to the edge of the asphalt. The smell of sulfur was in the air. Ahead of us was a flat area with scattered trees, then a large boardwalk. People were standing, their backs to us, watching a plume of smoke spit and sputter, as it rose a foot or two from the Earth. Excitement was in the air. Children were playing and calling to each other. Adults were laughing and talking with enthusiasm.

We were all there for the same reason: Old Faithful, the famous geyser in Yellowstone Park, which "faithfully" erupts approximately every 91 minutes. Based on our watches, we were just moments from seeing the next display. Here it comes! More spitting, but this time longer and reaching a few feet into the air. A pause, then more water and steam shot higher. Another pause. The crowd became restless.

Then Old Faithful came to life! Conversations stopped and children turned from their playing. With a swooshing sound, a stream of water and smoke rose from the opening in the Earth's crust. Forty feet, eighty feet, she kept rising higher. In less than a minute, she was well over 125 feet into the air as the steady stream of boiling water pushed up from the thermal underground. As quickly as she came, she dropped back into the ground. Little puffs of smoke popped out of the hole where gallons of water had shot out, just moments before. The geyser settled in to wait. In 91 minutes we would see her show off again.

That is how God is for each of us. He is faithful. He is always on time, never late. Even when we think He will not work in our lives, He is already doing things. Sadly, they may not be the things we want or think we need. He knows best and is working on our behalf.

Habakkuk 2:3

For still the vision awaits its appointed time; it hastens to the end—it will not lie. If it seems slow, wait for it; it will surely come; it will not delay.

God, why do I doubt You? Why do I feel I have to do things my way? When I look at the example of a simple geyser, timed so perfectly, why do I doubt You? Help me to slow down and see how perfect Your timing is. I want to wait on You and live my life for You. Thank You, Lord, for Your timing in my life.

May 4

King James

Edinburgh Castle stands on a hill. Thick stone walls surround the castle as tall and protective as they were designed several hundred years ago. Lush green valleys rise to the base of the hill. Within the fortress are small, flower-filled gardens, tucked away from wide pathways where carriages and other large entourages travel. The stone interiors of each room are cool, yet well-lit from the many delicate panes of glass adorning the room.

Mary, Queen of Scots lived and reigned here. She was a strong woman, known to have a head removed if the person was not loyal enough to meet her standards. Married to Lord Dudley, she gave birth to a son, naming him James. James' father died when he was only 8 months old.

At the age of 13 months, he became King of Scotland. Schooling was mandatory for him; he learned to speak several languages fluently. His religious training was mainly Presbyterian and Calvinist political doctrine. He grew up with many nannies and guardians. Some mistreated him, while others completely abused him. His mother was beheaded before he was 21 years old. As an adult he married and had eight children. Only three survived their infancy.

Standing in the small bedroom where he was born, it is difficult to imagine that this man, from such great sadness and loss, went on to produce the most-read book in the world. This is King James, the man who commissioned the Authorized Bible in 1611, which we still read to this day.

1 Peter 1:7 (of course our scripture is from the KJV)
That the trial of your faith, being much more precious than of gold that perisheth, though it be tried with fire, might be found unto praise and honour and glory at the appearing of Jesus Christ.

Lord, oh Father, how humble I feel seeing the life that this man lived. How can I say thank You for loving and protecting me? Words fail me, as I realize how You used a man with so much adversity in his life to achieve so much. I have not suffered like him, but I do want to be used by You, as You used him. Raise me up, Lord, to be the Godly person You want me to be. Let me look at my challenges and see the positive You have for me. Thank You, Lord.

May 5

The Alley

Walking the cobblestone streets of Assisi, Italy, I come upon a short side road: an alley. It is narrow enough for a grown man to stand in the middle, stretch out his arms and touch each side. There are three doorways on each side and one at the far end. Soft yellow walls of stucco glow in the twilight. The buildings are two stories tall, giving a tunnel-like feel to the space.

A slender weeping willow tree grows through a crack in the broken stone walkway. Dark, shadow-like branches hang low. There is no breeze to ripple through them, they hang waiting. Each doorway is different. The first one is a typical square frame, with a reddish-brown wood door. It boasts four simple panels. The next has an arched entryway. In dark chocolate brown wood, the door stands as a fortified barrier. Metal hinges and the handle look like they came straight off of a medieval castle.

The next door, a large panel of delicate carved wood, greets its guests. Within that panel is an entryway that feels Middle Eastern. Rounded at the top, the door itself is inset from the outer wall. Above each doorway, a dark metal light hangs, tall and narrow. The light is suspended by a matching metal chain, which is attached to a short pole sticking out of the wall; they are consistent in their style and coloring. Walking away from my alley, I wonder what made me stop. What caught my eye?

Then I get it. Each person on earth is like those unique doorways. Some are fancy, while others are very detailed. Still others are simple, straightforward. No matter our style, we are all covered by one Light: The light of Jesus Christ. He is over us, watching, guiding, and protecting our every move. He shines light onto our pathways, showing us our sins and leading us from them. He is our Light in whichever alley we choose to walk.

John 8:12

When Jesus spoke again to the people, he said, "I am the light of the world. Whoever follows me will never walk in darkness, but will have the light of life."

Jesus, thank You for being my consistent light. I know You are always with me, sometimes shining soft, while other times bright so that I can follow. I want to grow, to understand You more so Your light will shine through me to touch others.

We Have Lift Off!

Chilly morning air greets us, as we leave our hotel and board the bus. No one cares because we were on a mission. This morning we will witness something few others get to see: a space launch. The air is clear, not a cloud in the sky. A light breeze is gently blowing, no problem for the launch there.

Our designated viewing area is miles away, across a lake from the launch pad. Loudspeakers in our area inform us as events happen: The crew has boarded the space shuttle; the arm has been pulled back, etc. The countdown began: 10, 9, 8 ... it continues as engines roared to life and clouds around the base of the rocket grow bigger and more colorful in the morning light.

At last! "ZERO! Ladies and gentlemen, we have liftoff!" The white and black arrow-shaped rocket is off the ground, turning a little as it climbs higher and higher, faster and faster it rises. It seems like only seconds, but it is soon gone, a trail of clouds, drifting away, is all that is left. The awe! The exhilaration! We just watched a vessel carry men and women into space. They would arrive at the space station in a few days, bringing supplies and relief to those orbiting right now.

Contemplating what I had just witnessed, I got to thinking about my father. He had been a school teacher in the '50s and '60s. He taught science. After his passing, I found one of his books that had a picture of Earth. The caption said, "This is what scientists believe Earth looks like from space." Fifty years later, men and women were living in a space station! Man has walked on the moon! We have sent research equipment to Mars! We have come so far, yet we still know so little about the universe surrounding us.

Genesis 1:7-8

So God made the vault and separated the water under the vault from the water above it. God called the vault "sky." And there was evening and there was morning the second day.

God, You are the creator of all things. I know You created the heavens and the earth. I can barely grasp the distance man has traveled in space, yet Your creation is so much greater than I will ever comprehend. You, my God, are an awesome God. Thank You for showing me Your creation, for letting me stretch to new horizons, and for allowing me to know You better.

May 7

Lady Liberty

Walking through Battery Park, I see the ferry boat far off in the distance, crossing the Hudson River. Excitement stirs within me. I'm going to see The Lady! On the way, we pass gardens filled with roses: red and yellow, pink with white trim. Their fragrance is lost in the dirt, pipes, and bright orange plastic fencing. Construction happens everywhere, I think to myself as we hurry by.

Taking our place in line, we must pass through a security screening. A large tent is waiting for the group of people who have completed the process. Here comes the ferry! The cry goes out. Children dance and wiggle, their voices becoming louder. We are going to see The Lady!

Boarding the boat, bumping into other vacationers, we climb the stairs to the upper deck. A few women are wearing green foam crowns, purchased from a street vendor in the park, replicas of the crown on The Statue.

The ferry boat glides through New York Harbor. Fresh sea breezes play with our hair, while the salty air tickles our noses. In front of us, the milky green statue becomes clearer. She holds her torch high into the air in her right hand. Her left hand grasps the tablet with the date July 4, 1776: the date America declared her independence. At her feet lies a broken chain, representing freedom from tyranny.

She was a gift to the United States from France in 1886. How beautiful she stands, her green copper finish aged to perfection. We were in a great position on the upper deck of the ferry to study her detailed beauty. We can see her draped gown, her spiked crown and once more, the chains at her feet, no longer attached to anything; she represents freedom.

Do you still have chains on your feet? Have you knelt before God and invited His son Jesus Christ to come live in your heart? When you do, those chains will be broken and you will be able to stand like Lady Liberty in full view of the world...free!

Galatians 5:1
It is for freedom that Christ has set us free. Stand firm, then, and do not let yourselves be burdened again by a yoke of slavery.

Father in heaven, Your son had chains shackling him in prison. You released him from them, just like You have released me. Help me to remember that no one and nothing can chain me down. I am free because of Jesus Christ. Thank You, Father for that truth and victory.

May 8

Hannibal

Cobblestone streets, smooth sidewalks, and white picket fences line the historic section of Hannibal, Missouri. We had come to pay our respects to Tom ... Tom Sawyer, that is. Having read the adventures of Tom and his friends, we were looking forward to seeing the town where Samuel Clemens had based these writings.

Sitting along the Mississippi River; caught between modern life and the fictional characters who "lived" here, the town is welcoming. Not knowing which character we have come to pay homage to, they are warm and friendly, cautiously waiting for the question: Where is ...

Where is the home of Tom Sawyer? Where is the cave in which he and Becky Thatcher got lost? Where is the graveyard he went to with Huckleberry Finn? And, of course, which fence is the one Tom got others to paint, instead of doing the task Aunt Polly had given him. The home is across the street, white wood, two stories with a dark green front door. Restored as close as possible to the style of 1845, the home is visited by thousands of guests each year.

The cave? It's on the mountain. Follow a narrow, winding road, covered by oaks and maples. A tunnel of trees leads up the hill. Boulders larger than a car lay in piles, or by themselves, shading themselves among the big leafy trees. Near the summit, more boulders. This time, in the sun. Climbing onto one, we can see the mighty, muddy Mississippi River below.

How many times had we read about the adventures Tom and his friends had on the river?

It was so much fun to explore this area, to see the places described in the make-believe lives of children over 150 years ago. Leaving the town, I realized we had just spent an entire day following in the lives of make-believe people. Do we follow after make-believe people in our daily lives?

Celebrities want us to follow them; it's great for their wallets, but where are they leading us? Authors want us to buy their fictional stories, drawing us into the world of make believe. Is it closer to God? The movie industry exists because we follow what they produce. Most of their productions subtly undermine our faith in God.

1 Corinthians 11:1

Be imitators of me, as I am of Christ

Lord, I know You created me. You gave me ears to hear and eyes to see. I need Your constant direction to use them wisely. It is so easy to justify following others. Forgive me for choosing the make-believe, the fantasy, and the falsehoods over Your word. I want to follow You. Help me to turn from things that don't matter to those that do.

Her Shell

Tintern Abbey was founded in 1131 and rests near the River Wye on the border of Wales and England. All that remains of her large structure is the shell. There is no roof, and there are no windows to complete her beauty. The skeleton of her former self is all that remains. Over the centuries, her marble-covered stone columns were stripped of their milky white finish, taken to other locations for use in a palace or church.

Standing next to the church in the grass-covered cemetery, it is easy to imagine how beautiful she once was. Her abandoned brown-gray stone walls, two or three stories high, reflect her original grandeur. Two levels of archways, one on top of the other, line the sides of the building supporting the stone structure, which reaches high above them.

Porticos cover both of the longer sides, supported by more archways. The main entrance appears to have held wide double doors, which were beneath a large round rose window. Of course, the glass is gone now, but the detailed sections of stone still showcase her original beauty.

Grass grows where marble flooring once lay. Our guide tells us it was green marble taken by a 'Royal,' for use in his castle. Walking around the grounds, I separate from the group to explore on my own. I realize that the design of the Abbey is in the shape of a cross. People have taken away the valuable pieces of her physical beauty, her outward adorning is gone, but her inner beauty still shows. The cross still shows. No one has destroyed that.

The Bible tells us that each of our bodies is a temple for the Lord. That means we are like the Abbey. Have we allowed raiding parties to come and steal our beauty? Are we letting our temple deteriorate by improper use? Are we caring for it, by feeding it good foods and good scripture? It is our choice.

Romans 12:1

Therefore, I urge you, brothers and sisters, in view of God's mercy, to offer your bodies as a living sacrifice, holy and pleasing to God—this is your true and proper worship.

Father, my body is a temple for You. Please forgive me for not taking good care of it. I want my temple to be beautiful for You. Help me to guard it from wrong things. I want to feed it good food and Your word. I love You, Lord.

May 10

God Provides

Magnificent purple mountains stand guard in Texas' Big Bend region. Cacti burst with yellow and orange flowers, as far as the eye can see, blanketing the desert floor as ground animals scurry across the sand. The sun rose high in the sky, as our bus group traveled across the long barren ribbon of highway, heading home. Noon arrived with no place to eat, just miles and miles of desert in every direction. Another hour brought us to a little town and a closed café.

At the visitor center, I asked for a place where I could get food for 38 hungry people. Making a phone call, they asked if my folks would eat bar-b-q beef sandwiches. Having no idea if they would or not, I said yes!

It was an incredibly old former gas station, now operating as a food quick stop. The old style pumps were still in the center island, and the owners had placed huge flat rocks where the cars parked by the pumps. Walking in, we saw a man at the cash register and his wife at the entrance to the "kitchen." Forming a line, we picked up our freshly made sandwiches, chips, sodas, and other snacks. We paid our bills and sat on the rocks outside. The food was good and the conversation lively. After lunch, we went inside and bought ice cream and cookies.

Making sure everyone was on the bus, I went back in the store one more time. The husband and wife were standing in the middle of their little shop, arms around each other's waists. I thanked them for being so gracious. With tears in his eyes the man gave me a huge bear hug and said, "No, we thank you. You are angels sent from God for us."

Back on the bus, I got to thinking about that couple. I truly believe the other restaurant had been closed because this couple needed the financial boost that our group provided them.

Philippians 4:19
And my God shall supply all your needs according to His riches in glory by Christ Jesus.

Lord, let me always be open for Your will. Let me be a humble part of Your plan, and show me when I can be used by You for others' good. I want to be an angel in someone else's life, to bless them and draw them closer to You.

May 11

The Fire Station

Standing in front of the tall red brick building in downtown Los Angeles, I couldn't help noticing that it did not match the surrounding high rises of glass and chrome. Built during the era of horse-drawn fire trucks, the doorway had been widened over the years to allow for larger and more motorized vehicles. Eventually, the building became unusable for modern fire trucks and new high tech equipment: It was no longer needed. Emptied out and rendered useless, it sat there. New buildings with fancy designs were built all around the old fire station.

People walked by, hardly noticing the great architecture of the red brick building. While the outside was ignored, the inside sat in silence, metal ceiling panels of silver-gray grew dusty, the old bronze pole, from the sleeping quarters above to the street level below, was tarnished. The big glass front door filmed over, no longer transmitting sunshine.

City fathers wanted to tear it down, but the historical society stood its ground. This building had history! After many meetings, it was agreed that the building would remain. The former glory of this fire station was restored and became a restaurant. Business offices were created in the upper levels, which now means that once more, this building has became useful. Sitting in the dining room, I look around at the dark wood paneling, little vases of flowers on each table. Delicious aromas come from the kitchen how nicely the building has been brought back to life.

Doesn't God do that with us? Sometimes, we feel worn out, abandoned, used up, maybe even rejected and left empty, not able to see the sunshine anymore. God does not see us that way. He sees a beautiful vessel of His creation, something He wants to use to bring His message to others. He sees our potential to be of good use. What do we have to do to restore that vessel of His? It is up to us to reach out to Him. He is waiting and will restore us.

Isaiah 38:16
Lord, by such things people live, and my spirit finds life in them, too. You restored me to health and let me live.

Lord, wash over me. Restore me to the beautiful, usable vessel You created. I want to escape the abandonment and rejection I have been dealing with and be used in love and glory for You. Take away the bitterness and emptiness so that I can see your Son in His light. Thank You, Lord, for creating me to be so much more than I could imagine. Use me to be what You want.

Golgotha

"Have you ever been to Golgotha?," the pastor who lived in Israel asked me at a gathering of Christians and Jews in Texas. "Yes. It is an amazing place to see," I replied. We discussed how clearly the reddish-brown rocks were shaped to create the image of a skull. Even in this generation, it is quite visible. He mentions how that location is outside the wall of Jerusalem near the Damascus Gate. At the time of Jesus, this was a well-traveled road. People from every country brought their goods past Golgotha and into the city. The words placed on the cross above Jesus' head were in three languages because there were people from so many places passing by. Pontius Pilate wanted to make sure everyone knew Who this was.

In more modern times, the area was used as a trash dump. Piled high with waste, clearing it was quite a project for its new owners who used it as a parking lot for buses. Grease and oil drippings from the buses covered the dirt at the foot of Golgotha. The pastor and I agreed it was sad that no one cared about this significant part of Christian history on the hill so close to them. The pastor and I smiled and moved in different directions, however, the lovely sound of his deep, yet gentle, voice, with a hint of Hebrew softening his question, lingered in my mind. On my way home, my mind kept returning to our discussion. Had I ever been to Golgotha?

Have I walked down the road as a foreigner? Have I passed by The Place? Did I read the sign that said, "Jesus, King of the Jews?" Have I stopped long enough in my Christian journey to really weigh the price He paid, as He died for me? Do I leave my dirt and grease there to cover His blood?

1 John 1:7 (ESV)

But if we walk in the light, as he is in the light, we have fellowship with one another, and the blood of Jesus his Son cleanses us from all sin.

Lord, forgive me for passing by, for not stopping to focus on The Cross. I know I have carried the garbage of my life and dumped it at your feet before, but this time, I am asking You to cleanse me. Take away the "trash" of my life, and wash me clean. Help me to grow closer to you each day and not "park" myself in waste. Thank You for loving me. Thank You for the cleansing You are doing in my life.

Dinosaur Sue

As we enter the largest natural history museum in the world, the Field Museum in Chicago, Illinois, the marble floors of the large building greet us and the echoes of children's voices bombard my senses. The Field Museum is a stately building from the outside, with broad steps leading to Romanesque columns, which support the upper levels. It deceives the eye and hides the volume of exhibits inside.

Halls larger than most museums branch off of the main lobby. Three floors extending deep into the building provide hours of viewing. Our guide suggested that we allow at least three days to see everything! We can't. Our time is limited, and our focus is clear. We came to see Sue ... and there she is! 42 feet long and 13 feet high. She is the most complete and the best preserved Tyrannosaurus Rex in the world. She was discovered near my hometown in the Black Hills of South Dakota by a woman named Sue Hendrickson in 1990.

Sue (the woman) saw a bone sticking out of the ground. It turned out to be a part of the vertebrae, or backbone. Upon excavating the entire fossil, it was discovered that the piece Sue had seen was bleached by the sun. The rest of the bones were brown, having lay hidden for centuries, absorbing minerals from the earth. Now on display in the museum, it is easy to spot that one tell-tale bone. Lighter than the rest, it holds a special place in history, the one in the light.

Matthew 5:16

Let your light shine before men in such a way that they may see your good works, and glorify your Father who is in heaven.

Lord, I want Your light to shine on me. Bleach out any darkness in my life. Forgive me for hiding things. My sins are many, but my heart is open. I want to feel the warmth of Your glow, Your light on my life so others will see You in me. Thank You for leading me into eternal light.

May 14

Spice Market

Narrow streets filled with big-city hustle and bustle led us to the parking lot. Crossing the street filled with motor scooters and small trucks, we arrive at the entrance to the spice market. Istanbul, Turkey, is home to the largest spice trade in the world. This location has been the center of that trade since the mid-1600s.

Walking along a well-worn asphalt path, we follow the crowd. Women scurry by in flowing robes, burkas of dark brown or black. Their downcast eyes are the only human element visible. The arched entrance is narrower than the path, causing a bottleneck. Crowds bump and squeeze past in both directions. It feels like we are entering an underground cave.

Arriving inside, I feel a sense of accomplishment ... I made it! There are no windows, only the lighting of dim fluorescent tubes twenty feet above the shuffling crowd. Walkways open wider; we no longer feel crowded. There are more than eighty spice shops within this market; most of them have display tables outside their open-air shops. Tucked tightly together, there is only a thin wall dividing one establishment from its neighbor.

Salesmen are friendly, standing at the narrow entryway to their shops, offering advice and samples. Young Turkish men, fluent in English, promote the value of their products, while the older men, the grandfathers, sit near cash registers at the back of the store. Between the men, young sellers and old money changers, an entire world exists. Culturally, the older men wear traditional outfits, while the young ones are more Western in their dress. The elders do not speak English.

Spices! Hundreds of colorful spices had been piled into individual bins, each one about twelve inches square. Shaped into tiny pyramids, paprika, cumin, cinnamon, dry mustard, and so many more, all wait to be weighed and packaged. As far as the eye can see, little stacks rise from the tables. Product from around the world is available, each with its own healing or beneficial qualities, waiting to go home with us.

Walking from one display to the next, I look at the colors: red and yellow, brown and white. Hey! That's a children's song! Jesus loves the little children of the world. Here it is so vivid. People from all walks of life, from all corners of the earth, all colors of skin, have come together under one roof. Each of us is loved equally by God, our creator.

We may not all worship Him, but one day, we will all bow before Him and confess that He is THE Lord of all.

Romans 14:11

It is written: "As surely as I live," says the Lord, "every knee will bow before me; every tongue will acknowledge God."

Father in Heaven, Your works are so mighty. Your beauty is so amazing. I bow before You right now, thanking You for calling my name and teaching me to worship You, the one True God. I pray for all of the souls who do not know You, yet. Bring them under Your watchful covering. Include them in Your colorful array of worshipers. I love You, Lord.

The Dining Room

High on a hill, the stone fortress has stood guard for centuries, home to kings and rulers. Now open to the public, the long line moves slowly through Edinburgh Castle in Scotland. Peeking into doorways and dressing rooms, we arrive at the center of the castle, Crown Square. Our guide leads us into the very large formal, dining room. There are more than 25 chairs on each side of the polished dark wood table. Studying the finish, I could not see any imperfections in the wood. Master craftsmen designed this important piece of furniture with great care. Dark wood paneling lines the walls. Paintings of past kings and queens solemnly stare at us from their gold frames.

Side tables, dark wood with intricate details down each leg, are in position along the walls: at the ready. The windows stretch from ceiling to floor, partially hidden behind dark, heavy, thick drapes. Elegance and class exude from every corner, yet the room does not feel warm.

I tried to imagine the events which had taken place here, the fancy balls with women in huge skirts or tight-fitting gowns, men dressed in their finest brocaded attire. How many times had it been used by men plotting and planning a bloody war, or the pillage and destruction of a neighboring village? How many evil plans took place here? We know there were many times, from the 12th century on, where evil was at the center of this fortress.

I Corinthians 10:21

You cannot drink the cup of the Lord and the cup of demons, too; you cannot have a part in both the Lord's Table and the table of demons.

Lord, the world is filled with evil. I want to drink from Your cup. I don't need a fancy or huge castle to meet with You. I just need a small corner or an open field. Your dining room will always be a safe haven for me, a place I can come as I am. Thank You for preparing the table in the presence of my enemies, where I am protected by Your love.

Glitz and Glitter

Looking out the window, our plane was flying lower and lower, preparing to land in Las Vegas. A company convention required my husband to come so we decided to make it a family vacation. Our two teenage foster daughters had never seen huge hotels and bright-colored flashing signs, the kind they were now seeing.

Wide-eyed and open-jawed, the girls walked close to our sides, as we entered the airport terminal. Slot machines line every wall and stand in rows down the middle of the walkway. Clang, clang, tinkle, tinkle ... someone has just won some coins and they are dropping into the metal coin tray. Lights flash on the winning machine; an employee walks over to make sure all is well. People mill about, while others hurry past, dragging their suitcases like children's toys.

Driving down "the strip," our rental car has all four windows down. The girls have their heads out, looking up, all the way up, to the top of the 20-plus story hotels. Each one of the casino/hotels has its own theme. The girls are fascinated by the large-scale, blatant assault on their senses. One casino is designed to look like an Egyptian pyramid, another like Venice, Italy, while yet another boasts elegant water shows.

Entering our hotel lobby, people are talking loudly. Several women can be heard laughing in different parts of the opulent building. Once more, we can hear the clang and tinkle of coins dropping into metal trays.

After settling into our room, the girls ask if we are going to "win," some money, too. We explained that many people come to play, but few go home with the money they brought. Even fewer win a great deal of money. Most people lose; some come back over and over, hoping that the next time will be their big win. It rarely happens. They keep leaving with less than they brought. That is where the money comes from to pay for the big buildings, the bright lights, and the employees.

Isn't that how so many of us are with life? We are attracted by the "get rich quick" mentality, the big, bright, flashing "things" of life. How would our lives change, if we turned our eyes away from the glamour and glitter and focused on Christ? We would win more often, and when there were rough patches, He would be there to guide us through.

Colossians 3:2

Set your minds on things that are above, not on things that are on earth.

Father God, You are my guiding light, my protector from all that is wrong for me. Help me to stay focused on You, to read Your word every day and listen to You. Thank You for dying on the cross and keeping me from being lost because I know, as long as You are with me, I have won the race.

Portland Head Light

Low, white buildings with bright red roofs sit at the base of the slender lighthouse, a white tower with a wide black ring encircling the top, just below the bright light, which warns ships to stay clear of this dangerous, rocky cliff. Commissioned by President George Washington, it was completed in 1791 and is the oldest lighthouse on the Maine coastline. Below the towering light sits the keeper's home, which has been turned into a delightful, informative museum. Several of the lenses which served in the tower are now on display. Up close, the glass light fixture is actually made of thick squares, placed at specific angles. As the light inside the enclosure shines through the glass pieces, the angled pieces reflect brightly out to sea. The Portland Head light can be seen by ships as a far as 24 miles away.

Sitting on the "head," or rugged cliff, above the surf, it is a photographer's delight. Having visited this lighthouse many times, I decide to venture out on the rocky cliff a little north of the light, for a truly different angle. Small gray-green shrubs bobbed and shuddered in the sea breeze. Even though the sky was bright blue and the sun was shining, the wind blew its chilly breath across the cliff.

Bracing my feet, turning my body against the wind, I raised my camera. Click! "Got it," I thought to myself. But in that instant, my mind recalled something in the picture that had not been there as I focused. Thinking a spot of water had splashed from below, I turned the camera to wipe it off ... nothing there! The lens was clean and dry.

I decided to "review" my picture, turning it to face me, I looked at the last shot. Yup! There it was: the spot! But wait ... it was a butterfly! In the split second it took to click the picture, the small yellow butterfly had passed close enough for the camera to catch the details in her wings, even the detail of her antenna. What a shot! How quickly my picture had changed.

Life is like that. We have it planned out so nicely: beautiful surroundings, tall doses of perceived protection, plenty of space in front of us. Then ... wham! Something close to us changes our direction: illness, job, family crisis, you name it. We need to make sure our feet are planted on solid ground, not the edge of a cliff. We need to stay focused on the Light, the Protector.

Psalm 18:2

The Lord is my rock, my fortress and my deliverer; my God is my rock, in whom I take refuge, my shield and the horn of my salvation, my stronghold.

Lord, You are my light, always shining Your light for me to see, never giving up. You are my rock, solid, safe and dependable. Standing on Your rock, my life will never be defeated by the enemy. I ask You to help others find You and not be turned away by something distracting their vision. Thank You for keeping me focused on You.

Gone Fishing

I was fortunate to have my mother travel with me on a cruise through the Panama Canal. This was a dream of hers, and I was honored to have her as a part of my group and share the experience with her. Mother shared a cabin near the front of the ship with another lady. Their window was recessed; it actually had a ledge on the outside. The night before we arrived at the entrance to the Panama Canal, a storm had blown through.

Waking in the morning, mother looked out their window to find a flying fish had landed and gotten caught on the window ledge. It could not escape so it died. We informed the cabin steward, who said there was nothing that could be done for two days; we were not going to be near land to have someone take care of it. We would spend one day cruising from one end of the Canal to the other and the next day we would be at sea.

Word spread through the staff and cruisers that mother and her friend had a dead flying fish in their window. Folks would knock on their door and ask to see it. The crew of the ship came to take a look, as well. It became an attraction, and mother loved the attention: not so much the dead fish, but she loved the attention. Finally, we arrived in Curacao, where one of the ship's crew put on a rope harness and washed the poor decaying flying fish into the ocean. It was a proper burial at sea.

Philippians 1:3

I thank my God every time I remember you.

Father, I thank You. You put me in places where I can help others make memories. Help me look for opportunities to be a part of Your perfect plan for myself and those seeking after You. Let me never forget all the things You do for me and Your never-ending blessings.

May 19

The Lodge

Lake McDonald lodge in Glacier National Park was built in 1913 with a Swiss chalet design; inviting, yet out of place in the mountains of Montana. The ground floor exterior is white-washed stone, while the upper two layers are covered in chocolate brown clapboard with white trim. A stately white chimney towers over the lodge, with smoke from her huge fireplace teasing our noses in the clear mountain air.

Built in the days of the railroad, when hotels were part of the train travel experience, the lodge quickly became a summer destination. Entering the lobby, huge dark wood logs provide cross-beam and column supports for the upper floors of the hotel. Sofas covered in "western" design fabrics are set in groupings with wooden chairs and rockers, all facing the six-foot wide fireplace.

Two workers come into the lobby carrying a five-foot log. The path is cleared of guests, and the area around the opening is prepared. Gently, they place this huge piece of wood on the burning embers. Much to the delight of children nearby, we hear the pop and hissing of new wood being tempered by fire.

The back side of the lodge opens onto Lake McDonald. Almost a mile wide and ten miles long, she is fed from the snow-covered Rocky Mountains surrounding her. Across the lake, we see where a forest fire destroyed acres of green trees, now just sticks, standing guard over new growth.

The lakeside entrance was originally the front door. In the days before cars dominated transportation, boats brought vacationers from the train station, up the length of the lake, to this secluded location. As we climb the steps from the lake, red geranium filled flowerpots offset the green and brown landscape. A babbling brook beyond the edge of the lodge draws our attention. Rocks and stones of all sizes become the musical instruments of the snow-fed water. Children excitedly call out to their parents; a fish has been spotted.

Psalm 91:4

He will cover you with his feathers, and under his wings you will find refuge; his faithfulness will be your shield and rampart.

Heavenly Father, You are my lodge. Warm and protecting, You keep me from all of life's elements. Help me to learn to come to You more, instead of staying in dangerous or bad circumstances. You are my shelter and protection. Thank You for always being there.

May 20

Broken Bones

Cruising through the Mediterranean Sea, our first port of call is the beautiful island of Santorini, Greece. There are no docks large enough for our huge cruise ship, so it is anchored in the bay. Guests are brought ashore in "tenders," which are small boats. To see the island properly, a bus tour is the best option. From the tiny dock, we are driven up the side of the mountain. From a switchback to a hairpin curve, the view becomes more stunning as we arrive at the top.

Looking off across the ocean, it is easy to see that we were sitting on the rim of a volcano opening, also known as a caldera. Other islands clearly belong to the same rim, creating a familiar ring, or circle. This one appears to have the largest population. Eventually, our tour finishes at the picturesque town of Oia, which sits like a crown jewel on the northern tip of the island. As we are stepping off the tour bus, one woman in our party slipped on the step and broke her big toe. We got her back to the ship's doctor, who confined her to a wheelchair for the rest of the trip.

A few days later, we were visiting the ruins of the Basilica of St. John, located in Ephesus, Turkey. Another one of our ladies was intent on taking a picture. She focused in and then decided to step closer. Her foot went off the step, and she fell, breaking her knee and leg.

Every evening, all sixteen members of our little group would meet for dinner in the main dining room. After the first accident, our waiter prearranged the seating for the foot that needed to stay straight. After the broken leg incident, we would arrive in the dining room to find two chairs set with pillows: one for the broken foot and one for the wounded leg. It was a challenge to serve our group, to say the least.

Looking back on a situation that could have ruined the cruise for everyone, I smile to think of all the silly things we did with our two wheel chaired ladies. Isn't that how we should be with our problems? We can get down in the dumps about something and have a miserable time, or we can pray or start singing praise music to our King. We get to make that choice.

Psalm 59:16

But I will sing of your strength, in the morning I will sing of your love; for you are my fortress, my refuge in times of trouble.

Father, thank You for my choices. I choose to praise You. Your word says You inhabit our praises so, if I praise You, then I know You are with me, right here, in my heart. I like that, Lord. I choose You.

May 21

Chairs

Oklahoma City appears to be like most big cities in the United States. It has a great deal of traffic, road construction, and the hustle and bustle of crowds: people with too much to do and too little time in which to accomplish everything.

In the middle of the rush and noise, on the main streets of town, there is a park-like area. Gently rolling, well-manicured green lawns support one hundred sixty eight tall, narrow chairs made of stone, glass, and bronze, each one bears a different person's name etched into the glass base. Each chair represents a person, a victim of the bombing who would not be going home to his or her family for dinner. The attack took place on this site in 1995.

There are several items that make up the memorial: the entrance gates, called "The Gates of Time," the "Reflecting Pool," the "Memorial Tree" and the "Memorial Fence." The ones that touched me the most were the empty chairs. How sad. An empty chair means someone is no longer here. In this case, they are sadly, gone forever. The simplicity of the chairs and the choice of materials create a dramatic feel to the loss.

As I walk among the chairs, I pray. I ask God to make sure everyone was well taken care of and that children who had grown up with an empty chair in their home would learn to forgive, to be an example to others of His forgiveness, His love, and His mercy.

Ephesians 4:32

Be kind to one another, tenderhearted, forgiving one another, as God in Christ forgave you.

Father, on the cross Your Son, Jesus hung. As he was dying, He cried out to You and said, "Father forgive them." Teach me how to forgive. Teach me to free myself of the hold the enemy has on me. You are a God of mercy and Grace, and I thank You in advance for the release I will have, as You take control of my life, allowing Your light to shine in the dark places, the places that have been away from You.

Covered Bridges

"Rumble, rumble, rumble," the boards on the old wooden bridge sang their song as we rode across, watching the river below. Built over a hundred years ago, the bridge was still used by locals in the surrounding countryside. Rusty orange paint with brown trim was accented by maple, oak, and birch trees decked out in their fall attire. So picturesque!

The river below was filled with rocks of all sizes. Some were large enough to cause the water to divide and go around; while others were so small they never rose above the surface. Still others were partially submerged, allowing their smooth rounded surfaces to glisten in the sunlight, as water dances across.

My eyes return to the old bridge. I wonder what that bridge had seen over the years. Horse-drawn carriages with ladies dressed in their finest outfits, sitting so proper, while men in top hats handled the reins? Model A cars, which scared the locals and spooked passing horses? How about the weather it had stood through? Rain, snow, hail, and violent winds. It has probably seen its share of misuse and damage, as well. Enduring broken and worn-out boards, neglect, and maybe even abandonment.

Its life was much like our lives, I realized. The damaged bridge, abused and neglected or, like the rocks in the water below, swallowed by our challenges, not able to rise to the surface. These are all aspects of our lives that we deal with on a daily basis.

What can we do to change this? Accept Jesus Christ as your personal Lord and Savior. Ask Him into your heart. Give each of your challenges to Him, and stop worrying about them. He is stronger than the bridge and will carry your burdens for you. You will become like the rocks in the river, round and smooth with no rough edges. Only God can do that in your life. Let him in and enjoy your new life.

Revelation 3:20

Here I am! I stand at the door and knock. If anyone hears my voice and opens the door, I will come in and eat with that person, and they with me.

Father, I ask You to come into my life. Even if I have asked You before, I am inviting You in on a deeper level. Please work on me and through me to be the type of person You want me to be. Help my rough edges to become smooth and my worn-out sections to be restored, board by board. Restore me, Lord.

May 23

Clanging Bells

Waterfalls spilled from white glaciers high in the mountains: massive, wide, and powerful, dropping thousands of feet to rocky river beds below. Shorter falls looked like thin ribbons twisting their way down the side of the deep-blue ice of the glaciers. Below, rivers of light green glacier silt bounced and tumbled over huge boulders, on their way to Alpine lakes.

The Alps of Switzerland hold beauty beyond measure. Rugged peaks are covered in snow year-round, while in the lower elevations, low green shrubs decorate the fields. Tiny purple, pink, and yellow flowers bob in the breeze. Brown and cream-colored cows chew their cud. Each cow is fitted with a large bell on a wide leather strap around their neck. As they chew, the bell makes a "gong" sound. Each farmer has a different size bell, giving a different sound to his cattle.

The cattle are not branded; owners know where the cattle are by listening for them. When I hear these bells, I think of a large wind chime. Bong, bong, bong. The master knows His cattle by the sounds they make. As followers of Christ, we are known by the sounds we make, as well. Are the sounds we make gentle, soft gongs, or are they rough, loud clanging bells? When we speak, is it pleasant to hear our voice? Do people want to lean in and listen, or are we harsh? Do we encourage one another in our words and deeds? Our desire is to draw

others to Jesus Christ. Words, and the way we say them, can be a deterrent or a welcome to others.

1 Corinthians 13:1-2

If I speak in the tongues of men or of angels, but do not have love, I am only a resounding gong or a clanging cymbal. If I have the gift of prophecy and can fathom all mysteries and all knowledge, and if I have a faith that can move mountains, but do not have love, I am nothing.

Father, You are my protector. Show me how to lead others to You. Let my words be Your words, both in volume and love. I want my voice to sound like You so others will see You in me. Thank You for loving me enough to let Your voice be heard through me.

Crater Lake

Sitting on a log in the shadow of tall trees, I push dry pine needles in little circles with my shoe. In front of me and down a steep incline are the deep blue waters of Crater Lake. I am technically sitting on the rim of an extinct volcano, looking into the caldera, the center, where lava and ash once spewed forth. As the volcano has been inactive for millions of years, I am comfortable on my log. The rim is complete; there are no roads, rivers, or streams flowing in or out of it. Water is replenished in the lake by snow and rain. Evaporation is the main way water leaves the lake. Pure, pristine, and deep, at just under 2,000 feet deep, the blue water is very dark because depth produces stronger colors.

Crater Lake is in southern Oregon and is part of the Cascade Range of mountains. Dark green pine trees cover the mountains in every direction. A ground squirrel scurries past, stopping to chatter at me, and then runs up a tree. There is silence, nothing but the light breeze in the trees, a soft whooshing sound. A crow caws in the distance; several others reply. Again, silence.

Across the royal blue waters, a small, sharply pointed island rises. With the sun shining on its gray surface, it looks like its namesake: Phantom Ship. Studying the island, it appears to move slowly, to sail. I know it isn't moving; it is an island. But in the morning light, it is playing the part, a part the early settlers must have seen as well.

When visiting nature as I am today, I am overwhelmed with the beauty of God's creation. How he created everything with perfect color, with perfect spacing and with perfect height. I pause and ask myself, if He created all of nature so perfectly and so beautifully, what was He seeing as He created me? I see my imperfections, and I know there are so many. But He does not. He sent His son Jesus Christ to die on the cross at Calvary, to take away my imperfections, my sin. The world, even nature, has imperfections. But God takes those imperfections and makes them perfect, just like us.

Psalm 8:4-6

What is mankind that you are mindful of them, human beings that you care for them? You have made them a little lower than the angels and crowned them with glory and honor. You made them rulers over the works of your hands; you put everything under their feet

God You are my God, and I will always worship You. You are so beautiful, and I know You created me in your image. Sometimes, it's hard for me to realize that I am as beautiful as other things in Your creation. Help me to always remember how much You love me. Help me to see myself through your eyes. I love You, Lord.

May 25

Deadwood

Growing up in the small town of Deadwood, South Dakota, we were aware of the history. Gold had been discovered in the creeks, rivers, and rocks of this area. Men from around the world came to Deadwood in 1875-76 hoping to be one of the few, to strike it rich.

Most went home empty-handed, if they went home at all. Men came to work the sluices, devices that sifted gold out of the sand in the creek beds. Hard work and low pay, if any pay at all, yet everyone kept looking for that big strike. With the gold rush came other businesses: saloons, stores, and banks.

Today, the old buildings still stand downtown, having been converted into hotels or eating establishments. Wild Bill Hickok met his demise here. He was a lawman, gambler, and gunslinger who always sat facing the door while playing cards in the saloons. His fateful mistake came when he visited an establishment where a card game was in progress. The only open chair was facing away from the door. Throwing caution to the wind, he took the chair. Having been dealt an excellent hand, he did not notice Jack McCall enter the room.

The name Jack McCall is well-known in the area. He has the reputation of killing a famous man. However, he was tried, found guilty, and eventually put to death.

This is my hometown. We all come from "hometowns" that carry unique stories. When we read the Bible, there are many stories that cause one to pause and think, just like this one. Isn't that why God allowed the stories to be there, to help us understand that nothing and no one is perfect? It is our job to seek after Jesus Christ, the One who is perfect. His reputation is unsoiled, pure, and beyond reproach. He is our example, not man.

Proverbs 22:1

A good name is more desirable than great riches; to be esteemed is better than silver or gold.

Lord, help me to learn to follow You, not man. I want to have a reputation others will want to follow, leading them to You. Keep me from sitting in the wrong places. Help me to read Your word and abide by the guidelines of Your word. I love You, Lord.

A Picture Is Worth...

My dear friend Judy lives in a rural area of Texas. I think she knows or is related to everyone in her town and surrounding area. One of her relatives lived near me and was diagnosed with terminal cancer. We knew for many years that this woman and her husband had wanted to take a cruise to Alaska so Judy and I planned the cruise and invited a group of friends to go with the couple. We told no one the real reason we were doing this because we wanted Judy's family to have this special time together.

They loved the Lord and found great delight in His creation. Whales swimming near the ship, a glacier calving, waterfalls and ferns, the world was there for them. Each day on the cruise, Judy and I took photos of this sweet couple doing things together. She would send the candid shots to the couple's adult children so they could enjoy their parent's last trip. The woman's health held up, and she was able to participate in everything she had wanted to see and do. Several months later, we went to her funeral.

Her family had taken many of the pictures we had sent them and created a memory book for the guests to sign. There were many smiles, as those attending the services were able to see the couple having so much fun together. What a blessing it was for my friend and I to sow seeds of joy into others' lives.

Psalm 73:24-26

You guide me with your counsel, and afterward you will receive me to glory. Whom have I in heaven but you? And there is nothing on earth that I desire besides you. My flesh and my heart may fail, but God is the strength of my heart and my portion forever.

Father, let me never take anything for granted. Let me treasure each day and each person You place in my path. Even if I don't understand why You have placed difficult people in my life, let me always remember that I am Your light, and I need to shine for You. When I am weak, You are strong.

May 27

A Slice of Heaven

Studying the little green steam engine, it looks incapable of making the climb from Lake Brienz to the top of Brienzer Rothorn in Switzerland. Boarding one of only two cars that would be making the climb, I notice the elevation marker by the ticket window. We are currently at 1,857 feet. The climb will take us to an elevation over 7,000 feet above sea level!

The whistle blows, steam billows out of the smoke stack, and we are off! Chug-chugging along, we round a bend and pick up speed. Each of the five short but dark rock tunnels give way to more spectacular scenery. Alpine meadows come into view, green rolling hills, dotted with gray rock outcroppings. Brown and cream-colored cattle stand near, or on the tracks requiring the train whistle to be blown once more. The huge cattle bells hanging from their necks create a song, like large wind chimes. Bong, bong, bong. Each family has a different size bell for their cows so each family has a tone recognized as their own. For those of us on the open cars of the train, it is delightful music.

As we continue to climb, we watch the lake shrink in size. However, it increases in beauty. The delicate flowers of the Alpine meadows dance in the light breeze, appearing to be everywhere, creating a frame for the lake below. Tiny purple, white, and yellow flowers, no bigger than the end of your finger dance and sway in the high mountain air: tossed by light breezes from above. Swiss Alps are hosts to many glaciers. As they slowly grind their way down rocky mountains, a very fine powder is created. As the edges of the ice melt, the glacier powder is carried to the lakes below. This powder reflects sunlight, causing the lake to shimmer in amazing shades of turquoise; almost milky, it looks soft, smooth, and silky.

This is a train ride of a lifetime! We are seeing beauty beyond measure, God's beauty, God's creation ...a little slice of heaven. I have a thought, "If this is a little slice, I can't even begin to comprehend what a full, big slice will be like!"

Are you prepared for His heaven? Are you right with Him? Do you want to wait until the last minute to get right and maybe miss your chance? Do it now. Invite Jesus into your heart; ask Him to forgive your sins and prepare a place like this for you in eternity.

Psalm 8:1

LORD, our Lord, how majestic is your name in all the earth! You have set your glory in the heavens.

Lord, you say You are coming soon to take us home to heaven. The thought of being with You in this kind of paradise is beyond my imagination. Thank You for loving me and showing me a little taste of things to come.

May 28

Queen Mary

Spying her black and white hull with three red smoke stacks, the RMS Queen Mary sits proudly in her permanent mooring in the Long Beach, California, harbor. Designed as a luxury sailing vessel, launched in 1934, she plied the waters between New York and England, transporting wealthy aristocrats and poor immigrants alike.

Entering the ship, we cross the wide, dark wooden floor of the promenade: a walkway that shades the upper decks, where guests could meet and mingle, yet not get burned by the North Atlantic sun. It was quite the gathering place during transatlantic crossings. Beautiful carpet greets us, as we open the doors to the interior. Patterns of gray, red, and cream blended together, subtle elegance. Highly polished dark paneling covers the walls. Occasional chairs sit in groupings, encouraging conversation. We are in the first class lounge, of course!

Small shops line the walkway to the bar in the bow of the ship. Above the smiling bartender is a mural depicting guests on board, dressed in their '30s and '40s gowns and suits. Dancing and laughing, they appear to have no worries. This is an original work of art, placed here before her inaugural sailing.

The first class dining room walls are lined with light shades of delicate wood. Intricate carvings are inlaid. Heavy drapes hang in long folds, pooling on the floor. Round tables are set with linen and fine china; they sit on dark red carpeted flooring.

Queen Mary did not always travel in this style. During World War II, she was re-fitted and used as an Allied troop carrier, ferrying armed forces to ports all over Europe. She was originally designed to carry several thousand guests; however, at the height of her service, she sailed into the New York Harbor with sixteen hundred men on board. Every day they each had three eight-hour shifts: one was out on deck, regardless of the weather conditions. Another was spent in their bunks ... "You'd better enjoy it because, in eight hours, someone else will kick you out!" The last eight hours were spent working: cooking, cleaning, washing, watching for enemy aircraft, it didn't matter, that was their shift.

After the war, the Queen Mary was refitted once more, returning to luxury cruising, until 1967, when she retired to sunny Southern California.

Psalm 107:23-24

Some went out on the sea in ships; they were merchants on the mighty waters. They saw the works of the Lord, his wonderful deeds in the deep.

Lord, sometimes I feel over-burdened, like the Queen Mary. I have too many things going on and feel like I can't handle them all. Thank You for showing me that, just like this beautiful ship, I can be used by You for many things. Put me to good use, help me to help others. I know that when it is time for me to retire and go to be with You, I will experience the shining glory of Your Son.

Which Way?

Taking people on vacation is my job. I travel all around the world with groups of people. Whenever possible, I try to visit the places before I take a group, making sure it will be acceptable and comfortable. For some time, I had wanted to take a group on a small ship up the Columbia River. The owner of the vessel, Jeff, called and said he had room for two. Calling my friend Judy, we quickly made plans. Jeff keeps his boat in Seattle and cruises in several directions from his home port. In our excitement, we completely forgot to ask where we were going!

He had asked us to fly into Seattle, instead of Portland, which is the city at the mouth of the Columbia River. Boarding the boat, we set sail. Heading north, it dawned on us that this cruise was not going in the anticipated direction of the elusive Columbia River. Instead, we went through the waterways surrounding the San Juan Islands and up the coast of British Columbia, Canada.

What breathtaking scenery! Rolling hills quickly became majestic mountains covered by forests of pine trees. Waterfalls flowed from craggy outcroppings. Inlets stretched for miles, deep into the mainland of Canada, with only the sound of our boat's engine and the gentle lap of the water against the bow of the boat. Sunsets reflected over the open ocean or filtered through tree-lined islands. Sea otters sunned themselves along rocky shores. God's beauty was everywhere. To this day, whenever we reflect back on this trip, all we can do is laugh. Two professional women in the travel industry did not even know where they were going, but what an amazing experience we had.

Isn't that what God asks of us, complete surrender to His will? We don't need to question Him. He has our lives in the palm of His hand ... if we let Him. We must choose to accept His direction, timing, and love. When we do, what unspeakable joy our lives will be.

Psalm 32:8

I will instruct you and teach you in the way you should go; I will counsel you with my eye upon you.

Lord, lead me in Your ways. Help me to stay focused on Your direction for my life. I know there are so many amazing things You want me to see and do, as I experience Your beauty. Thank You for loving me and allowing me to lead others to You.

Never Enough Patriotism

Sitting on the edge of the open prairie, distant mountains covered with forests of dark Ponderosa pine trees, make them look black. The Native Americans who have lived here for generations gave these mountains the name "Black Hills." Walking along the evergreen-lined paths, the fragrance of pine needles fills the clear crisp air, tingling the senses. Birds chirp in the trees, while little gray ground squirrels scurry here and there in search of food. The Black Hills are home to hundreds of clear cool babbling brooks, filled with fly fishermen angling for the perfect trout.

Mount Rushmore is my focal point. Gazing at the four granite faces of Presidents; Washington, Jefferson, Roosevelt, and Lincoln, I realize what a patriotic location I am visiting. Motorcycle groups enjoy visiting the Black Hills to ride through rolling hills, past picturesque rock outcroppings with names like "The Cathedral Spires" hoping to catch a glimpse of mountain goats, bison, bighorn sheep, and wild turkeys. Many of the bikers are veterans from our current and past wars.

One year, I was sitting near the viewing area watching visitors from around the world come and go. Sometimes, I would volunteer to take a picture of a family struggling to get everyone in a shot. Other times I just smiled at the folks as they went by. I watched three men approach the viewing area. They were obviously bikers, clomping towards the viewing area in their black leather boots, chains dangling from their back pockets, and the requisite leather vest with patches on the front and back.

I turned away and then turned back to see what the "bikers" were up to. They were facing the sculpture, standing perfectly still, close together, arms across each other's shoulders. Just standing. No movement for several minutes. Finally, they turned and walked away. Tears were in their eyes, as they passed by. I looked at their backs and realized that the patches on their vests were that of Vietnam veterans.

My first reaction when I see a Vietnam vet is to thank them and welcome them home, as they did not receive a "welcome home" upon their initial return. Watching them go by, there were no fancy clothes, no showy entrance, no public displays. They came to pay respect to the freedom they believed in and fought for, to seek comfort from our past great leaders.

I think about these men and the respect they are paying. How often do I stop and pay respect to my Lord. Do I only do it on Sunday morning with the rest of my church family, or do I thank Him for the freedoms He gives me on a daily, even an hourly basis.

Matthew 6:33

But seek first his kingdom and his righteousness, and all these things will be given to you as well.

Jesus let Your cross be ever in front of me, as my symbol of Your victory for my life. Let me never underestimate Your love and the victory You have given me.

A Walk with Him

Stepping out of my car, deep in the woods of Canada's YoHo National Park, I could hear the thunderous sound of the massive waterfall, before I could see her beauty. Rain had drenched the area a few hours ago, leaving the sweet aroma of damp pines to tickle my senses. Walking a few short steps, I peered over the cliff into the valley to see the raging river, hundreds of feet below. Mist was rising off the trees on the other side of the valley, giving a mystic quality to my surroundings. Standing there, admiring God's beauty, I lifted my face and hands toward heaven and began to sing an old song of the church: "Oh Lord, My God, when I in awesome wonder, consider all the worlds Thy hand has made ..." I began to weep, overcome by His mighty creation, knowing that I was a part of these works.

I heard a gentle voice call my name. Opening my eyes and looking around, I saw no one. Thinking it was simply noises in the trees, I wiped my eyes, preparing to climb back in my car and continue the journey. But wait. There it was again, this time more distinct, "Susan." Turning towards the cliff, I took in the full glowing beauty of my Lord. He was above the trees, appearing to float. The white clouds that had been rising from the trees only minutes before did not match the glorious purity of His Presence.

Walking to the edge of the cliff, my entire being was focused on Him. "Yes Lord?" He reached His hand towards me and said, "Come to me." Without hesitating, I stretched my hand to Him and began to walk. I didn't think about the many reasons I should not walk off a perfectly good cliff, into the deep abyss below. I wanted to be near Him, feel His unending pure love, and be obedient to His calling. Looking into His face, which exuded peace and joy, nothing else mattered.

After walking several yards, far above the treetops, I took my eyes off of Him for a split second. Wow! Here I was, walking so far above the trees and the raging river below! How awesome am I? Yes, look at me, look at what I am doing! Those are the thoughts that raced through my mind.

Just as quickly, I began to fall. Like a rock, I was falling through the air towards the treetops far below. Looking up at Christ, my arms still reaching towards Him, I cried out for forgiveness. Forgive me for my self-centeredness, my ego, my selfishness, and my choosing to not trust You completely. My falling stopped. His hand engulfed mine again, and He gently pulled me closer. It was then that I realized how simple His request of me is: Keep my eyes focused on Him, and He will provide for my needs and desires.

I remembered the story in Matthew 14: 28-32. The disciples were in a boat on the Sea of Galilee. Jesus walked to them on the water. Peter asked the Lord to walk on the water with Him. Jesus said, "Come." Peter climbed out and began to walk towards Christ. He looked at the storm swirling around them and began to sink. Asking for his Lord to save him, Jesus lifted him up.

In an instant, while I was remembering that story, Jesus walked me back to the cliff and disappeared from my sight. He had left me physically, but His presence was still all around. The waterfall was still flowing, the mist was still lifting. God was still here. Remembering the scripture, I compared it to this experience God had just given me. All of a sudden I needed to know what happened to Peter. I knew he didn't drown, but what happened? My Bible was in my car. Flipping through the pages, I found the story and the conclusion. Simply stated, it says, "and when they got in the boat together, the storm ceased."

Wow, Lord, how simple are Your teachings? "When they got in the boat together, the storm ceased." Thank You for showing me Your beauty in the forest and letting me see that Your abiding love is ever present. Help me to keep my eyes focused on You so that I do not fall. Let others see Your Glory and beauty as they focus on You, as well.

Lord, let us stay in Your boat together.

I pray you

will find a new and closer

relationship with our

Lord Jesus Christ

through these devotions.

HE simply wants

your heart!

May God continue to

shower blessings

upon you as you learn

to trust Him more, each day.

For your reading pleasure

and your

daily time with the Lord, Jesus Christ.

Collect the series:

'Summer'

'Autumn'

and

'Winter'

Devotional Editions

To place your order,

Contact:

Susan Howell

www.susanchowell.com

Vacations Unlimited

210-308-8500

4091 De Zavala Road

San Antonio, Texas 78249

38514322R00119

Made in the USA
Charleston, SC
09 February 2015